PRESUMPTUOUS

PRESUMPTUOUS

Living Beyond Limits, Labels, & Logic.

ANDREW C. JAMES

SUMMERHILL
PUBLISHING

ISBN: 978-0-9953000-8-8 (Hardcover)
ISBN 978-0-9953000-9-5 (Paperback)

First Edition

Published in Canada
Summerhill Publishing
Shelburne, Ontario

Cover Photo: Tristan Barrocks

andrewcjames.com

Dedicated to the only one uniquely qualified to live this presumptuous life with me, Juli-Anne.

∏P

"If perception shapes reality, then transformation begins with how you perceive your perceptions."

-Andrew James

Table of Contents

Foreword

Alright, let's get this out of the way—I don't usually write forewords. But when my brother-in-law, Andrew, asked me to do this, I didn't hesitate. Not because I had nothing better to do (trust me, I do), but because this book? It's something special. And so is the guy who wrote it.

If you know Andrew, you know he's always been a little... extra. Not in a bad way, just in that way where he refuses to believe something can't be done. Where most people see a door closed, Andrew is the guy looking for the window, the side entrance, or just deciding to build his own house instead. He calls it being presumptuous. I call it just being Andrew. And honestly, it's worked out pretty well for him.

I get it, though. Living a presumptuous life isn't just something I've watched Andrew do—it's something I know first-hand. The music industry isn't exactly a place for people who like to play it safe. You have to be bold, trust your instincts, and move with conviction, even when the path isn't clear. You have to be willing to take risks, to believe in the impossible, and to push past every doubt and every "no" that comes your way. And that's exactly what this book is about.

Andrew's life has been one big, audacious leap after another.

He's started businesses with no business starting them, built a community hub with nothing but faith and determination, and somehow convinced my sister to marry him—which, if you ask me, was his boldest move yet. And now, here he is, writing a book about how you, too, can live a life where you dream big, push past doubt, and make things happen.

This book isn't some fluffy motivational piece where you're told to "believe in yourself" and call it a day. Andrew lays it all out—his wins, his missteps, the lessons he's learned along the way. He's real about the challenges, the moments of uncertainty, and the faith it takes to keep moving forward when things don't go as planned. And through it all, you see one undeniable truth: living a presumptuous life isn't about waiting for the right moment. It's about moving, trusting, and figuring it out as you go.

So, here's my advice—read this book. Let Andrew's stories push you to think bigger, take action, and stop waiting for permission to go after what you're meant to do. And if, at the end of it all, you still think playing it safe is the better option... well, just know that Andrew would strongly (and loudly) disagree.

Enjoy the ride.
Noel Cadastre

Preface

I recently had the opportunity to speak at a career day at a local high school. The organizers of the career day asked me to share my story because they felt my unconventional perspective would be of value to students at such a critical decision-making time in their lives. They understand how important it is to expose young minds to alternative paths—beyond the traditional route of a diploma, a "stable job," and climbing the corporate ladder.

After sharing my entrepreneurial journey and life experiences, a student boldly said, "I just want to make money. Money is my motivation." Her comment stuck with me. Honestly, it became one of the driving forces behind this book.

That mindset wasn't new to me. In my over 25 years of working with youth, I've seen it many times. The allure of quick money often eclipses the pursuit of purpose. While it's understandable—especially in a culture that glorifies material success—this mindset often leads to thoughtless career choices and a lack of true fulfillment. It also makes young people especially vulnerable to shortcuts that promise fast money—like drug dealing and other traps that *ultimately cost more than they give.*

Throughout my life, I've experienced over and over the reality that following the lead of your purpose provides infinitely more fulfillment than simply chasing a paycheck. Purpose-driven choices opened doors to unexpected and rewarding opportunities, and my unconventional journey has been filled with experiences that enriched my life in immeasurable ways.

That's how I know that it's okay to deviate from the norm, take risks, and trust your instincts. When you align your pursuits with your purpose and values, you not only achieve personal fulfillment but also make a meaningful impact on the world around you.

Whether you're still in high school, or you've already passed through those early decision-making years, the principles of living a presumptuous life are relevant. Regardless of your age or stage in life, it's never too late to realign yourself. The desire to live a life of meaning, to break free, and to pursue a path that resonates deeply with who you are, doesn't have an age limit. Whether you're seeking a new direction, reviving an old dream, or simply striving for greater fulfillment, this book offers the inspiration to help you embrace your presumptuous life.

Preface

My journey of living an authentic, presumptuous life has been deeply rooted in a desire to do my own internal work. It's this commitment to personal growth and self-discovery that has allowed me to navigate my path and empowered me to live freely. Recognizing the importance of this internal work is essential for anyone striving to live a life of purpose and boldness.

With this book, I hope to provide you with truth that liberates you from places where you have been unjustly held, so that you can achieve your true potential and live your real life.

So let's embark on this exploration together, and I pray you are empowered to take hold of your presumptuous life with bold steps, brave choices and boundary-breaking actions.

Acknowledgements

This book is the result of years of learning, growing, failing, and getting back up again. I could not have done it alone, and I wouldn't want to.

First, I give thanks to God—my source, my strength, and my guide. Every step of this journey has been marked by His grace, and it is only by His wisdom that I have anything of value to share.

To my wife, Juli-Anne—thank you for your unwavering support, your sharp editorial eye, and your belief in this message. You took my thoughts, refined them, and made this book stronger than I could have on my own. More than that, you are my greatest encourager and the one who constantly pushes me to be better. I am eternally grateful and eternally yours.

To my daughters, Akeylah, Amaya and Alexandra—you inspire me every day. Your curiosity, creativity, and courage remind me why it's so important to live with purpose and integrity.

To my dad and extended family—thank you for the foundation you laid in my life, the lessons you taught me, and the love you continue to show. Your support has been a steady anchor throughout my journey.

To my mentors, friends, and those who have spoken into my life—you may never fully know the impact of your words and actions, but I do. Your encouragement, challenges, and wisdom have shaped me in ways I cannot put into words.

To the incredible teams at Streams Community Hub and Town Tees—our staff, board, volunteers, students, and supporters—thank you for being part of this wild, faith-filled adventure. The work we do together reflects the very principles in this book. Your dedication, creativity, and belief in the mission push me to keep going, even on the hardest days.

And finally, to you, the reader—thank you for taking the time to engage with these words. My hope is that they encourage, challenge, and equip you in ways that go beyond these pages.

With gratitude,
Andrew Charles James

The Courage
to be
Presumptuous

You know that moment when something clicks—when what you once thought was impossible suddenly feels like destiny calling?

That happened to me at five years old, lying on the carpet, watching Michael Jackson glide across the stage with a move the world had never seen. The moonwalk didn't just entertain me—it unlocked something inside me. I didn't have language for it then, but I would later come to understand it as the beginning of a bold new way of thinking.

It was the day I learned that limits are often lies.

But for most of my life, I've been called something else for thinking that way.

Presumptuous.

PRESUMPTUOUS

It's a word that, for many, drips with negativity—conjuring images of arrogance, overstepping, or acting entitled. You hear it in tones of rebuke, not celebration. Someone who "does too much," "moves too fast," or "assumes too much."

But I want to challenge that. In fact, I want to reclaim it. Because when the world tells you to stay in your lane, play small, and follow the rules—even when those rules aren't working for you—what do you do?

You either shrink... or you get presumptuous.

The Latin root of the word presumptuous is *praesumere* — "to take before." In its truest form, it means to boldly assume something is possible—even before there's evidence. And what is faith, if not exactly that?

That's what this book is about. It's about the courage to believe before the blueprint. To act before approval. To speak before validation. To live in alignment with your God-given purpose—even if the world calls it unreasonable.

This is not a how-to manual. It's not a motivational speech in book form. It's a lived journey. I'll share the moments that shaped me—from the classroom to the stage, from failure to breakthrough, from the basement to the storefront, from faithless wandering to Spirit-led clarity. Some stories will make you laugh. Others might challenge how you've seen yourself. All of them are meant to do one thing: call out the bolder, braver version of you.

Because here's the truth: the presumptuous life isn't for the few. It's for the called. And if you're holding this book, you've already heard the whisper—*there's more.*

So let me offer this: Presumptuousness, when rooted in purpose and tethered to faith, is not arrogance—it's obedience.

The dictionary defines presumptuous as "failing to observe the limits of what is permitted." But here's the question: Who decides what's permitted? Culture? Family? Fear? Or God?

To live a presumptuous life is to step boldly beyond the limits imposed by fear, doubt, and convention.

We're going to walk through the seven pillars of a presumptuous life—integrity, discipline, conviction, action, joy, agility, and faith—and I'll show you how they've shaped me. Not in theory, but in real life. Through decisions, detours, and defining moments.

By the end, I pray you'll be emboldened not just to dream

bigger—but to move, speak, build, lead, and believe differently.

Because the world doesn't need more safe.

It needs more bold.

It needs more presumptuous.

It needs you.

How to Use This Book

At the end of each chapter, you'll find a section called **Presumptuous in Practice**. It's not just for reflection—it's built to help you *live* what you've just read. Each one includes:

- 💡 A **Reflect** prompt to help you pause and take inventory
- ✍ A **Journal Prompt** to go deeper
- ▶▶ A **Bold Move** to put it into action
- 💡 And a **Reframe** to shift your perspective

You can work through them as you go or circle back at the end—but don't skip them. This is how you start walking it out.

1
___

Starstruck

¶|P

I t's three months before my fifth birthday—the day that everything changed: May 16, 1983.

I'm lying on my stomach on the family room floor, my hands under my chin, my elbows propping me up. My eyes are fixed on the television screen. I didn't know what was coming, but something in me was waiting—expecting the extraordinary.

And then, it happened.

He stood still, poised, his energy electric. And then—he moved. Or did he? His body moved like a contradiction—backward motion with forward intent—defying every natural law we'd come to accept.

It was mesmerizing. A defiance of human limitation. **The moonwalk.**

That single moment didn't just amaze me—it shifted something in me. It cracked open the door to a new way of thinking, where the impossible wasn't a wall, but a challenge waiting to be overcome.

I hold a firm belief that in my formative years, God used Michael Jackson as a vessel to ignite a profound sense of purpose in me. MJ's iconic moonwalk at the Motown 25 anniversary wasn't just a performance—it was a portal into a new reality, where possibility felt infinite.

The way I saw it, he had done something that was factually impossible—until the moment he did it.

Impossible, that towering giant, suddenly looked a lot smaller. Less intimidating. Less worthy of fear. I understood that I could simply convert him to possible, if I wanted to.

That early encounter made me bold—bold enough to think differently. It made me steadfast in a conviction that nothing was impossible. Or, perhaps more accurately, impossible was nothing. I learned that most barriers are perceived, and those perceptions are just illusions, waiting to be shattered by my will and faith.

As I continued to grow, I experienced numerous undeniable

God-moments: moments that affirmed and reaffirmed this truth. Every experience was another drumbeat of proof. Since childhood, I've marched to the beat of that drum, not swayed by things like societal norms and parental expectations. I learned that conviction mattered more than permission. That doubt and naysayers would always be there—but they didn't have to define my path.

Long before I had language for purpose or possibility, I was already practicing it—in the simplest ways. My tools weren't profound. But they were enough to start shaping a world I believed in.

Cardboard, Masking Tape & Scissors

Some of my earliest memories involve playing with cardboard—my first canvas for creativity. I created elaborate worlds, gadgets, and games, each more ambitious than the last, believing in my ability to bring my imagination to life. While my childhood creations may have been crude by adult standards, they were significant in building my belief that I could shape my own world and destiny, just as I shaped those cardboard creations.

I believe that we humans are powerful beyond measure and there is nothing we can't do if we believe we can. Of course, this kind of power can very easily lead to over-confidence and arrogance. But power given by God—and submitted to God—ensures we don't place our assurance in ourselves. That's how our faith becomes audacious—even presumptuous—not rooted in wishful thinking, but in divine alignment. It is tethered to a creator and a master plan that we are bravely seeking to discover. So, we can embrace the unknown with joy, courage, and conviction, knowing that even in the face of failure, there is direction, growth, and resilience to be found. We can dare to dream big and refuse to settle for mediocrity, knowing that the pursuit requires faith, audacity, and tenacity.

What Do You Believe Is Possible?

Before any discussion about the pillars of a presumptuous life begins, I need to ask you—what do you believe is possible?

I ask this not as a rhetorical question, but as an invitation to stretch your imagination, to unshackle your mind from the chains of "realism" and "practicality" that so often bind us. What if the very things you've dismissed as out of reach were simply waiting for you to reach out? What if the impossible was merely a veil, thin and fragile, just waiting for you to tear through it?

As you think about this, remember that the journey to the impossible begins with a single step of audacity. The moonwalk was that step for me—a simple yet profound shift in how I viewed the world and my place within it. And now, I urge you to find your own moonwalk moment, that spark which ignites the flame of possibility within you.

So, I ask again—what do you believe is possible? Because knowing what's possible is just the beginning.

Living it out requires integrity—the kind that shows up when no one else is watching. That's where we're going next.

Presumptuous in Practice

○ **Reflect:** Think back to a moment in your childhood that sparked awe, wonder, or inspiration.

✎ **Journal Prompt:** What do you currently believe is *impossible* in your life? Write it down—then challenge it. What would it take for that to become possible?

▶ **Bold Move:** Choose one "impossible" thing this week and take one small step toward it.

💡 **Reframe:** What if what moved you deeply was designed to move you forward?

dlb

2

Only Say
What You
Can Own

¶|P

It was an ordinary day—just like any other. I was ten years old, in Grade 5, huddled at recess with a group of kids, laughing and joking like we always did. I was caught up in the moment, when one of my friends made a bad joke about another classmate who wasn't around to defend himself. Without thinking twice, I joined in with my own comment.

At the time, it felt harmless—just kids being kids, right? But I had no idea I'd have to own those words sooner than I thought.

Later that afternoon, the classmate we'd been joking about found me. His face told me everything—he was hurt, angry, and disappointed.

"Did you say that about me?" he asked, his voice trembling.

I had a choice to make. I could lie, play it off with humor, or own up to what I'd said.

I chose to own it—completely.

"Yes," I said, looking him in the eye, remorseful but honest.

His reaction caught me off guard. It was a mix of shock and, maybe, a little relief. He was surprised—because, let's be real, how often does a kid admit to doing something wrong? But I think he was also relieved—he could see I wasn't trying to cover it up or make excuses. What followed surprised us both—we had a real, honest conversation. It wasn't easy, but it was one of those moments where we both grew a little.

That day, I learned a powerful lesson about integrity—about how our words and actions carry real weight. I made a promise to myself that day: I wouldn't say anything I couldn't own up to if someone confronted me. Whether my words were good or bad, I needed to be able to take responsibility for them. That decision became a guiding principle in my life, shaping not just how I interacted with others, but how I viewed myself.

Looking back, it would've been easy to lie, to avoid the awkwardness or the fallout. But even then, I knew how important integrity was. If I started lying about small things, where would it lead?

I've known people who convince themselves that small lies don't matter—that they're harmless. But lying always starts small, and it always starts with others. Eventually, though, you start lying to yourself. And that is the most destructive kind of deceit. Because if you can't be honest with yourself, how can you expect to live a life of integrity? A true, free life—one not just built on values, but built to add value.

Integrity in the Small Things

Integrity isn't just about big, defining moments—it's about the small, everyday choices that build your character. It's about being honest in your interactions, keeping your promises, and doing the right thing, even when it's tough or inconvenient.

As I grew older, this lesson in integrity became part of me. It has served me well in countless situations. Whether starting a new business venture, mentoring a young person, or facing a personal challenge, I strive to make sure my words align with my actions.

Living a presumptuous life—a life where you take bold risks and chase big dreams—requires a strong foundation of integrity. Without it, everything else is at risk of crumbling. Integrity ensures that what you're building is stable and sustainable. It's the anchor that holds everything together, even when life's waters get rough.

Living with integrity isn't easy. In fact, if you're doing it right, it'll sometimes be excruciating. But it's always worth it. Integrity gives you the confidence to stand tall, knowing you're being true to yourself and your principles.

It's what lets you sleep at night—knowing you did your best to live in alignment with who you are and what you believe. And when you know you've missed the mark, integrity keeps you self-aware enough to admit it—and honest enough to correct it.

Taking Inventory

As you reflect on the role of integrity in your own life, I encourage you to take inventory. Think about the promises you've made—to others, and more importantly, to yourself. Are you keeping them? Do your actions align with your words—and the values you say you live by?

The pursuit of more—whether success, fulfillment, or the presumptuous life you dream of—demands a high standard. You cannot truly achieve more if you're not willing to own your words and actions, both in public and in private.

It's easy to put on a show for others, to project an image of integrity. But the real test is how you live when no one else is around. Are you living in a way that's authentic, where your inner life matches your outer life?

The truth is, integrity is a lifelong journey, not a destination. It's not about achieving perfection, but about striving to live honestly and authentically every single day. It's about embracing the small, seemingly insignificant moments of truth that, when added up, define who you are and how you'll be remembered.

Living with integrity is a lifelong process—where every decision moves you closer to freedom, purpose, and a life that's truly yours. And that, in the end, is the most daring and rewarding journey you can embark on.

And if integrity anchors us, discipline propels us. Now that we've looked inward, let's explore how we push forward—even when it hurts.

Presumptuous in Practice

Reflect: Reflect on a recent situation where your integrity was tested.

Journal Prompt: Make a list of unspoken or broken promises (to others or yourself).

Bold Move: Choose one and make it right this week.

Reframe: Ask: Am I living a life I'd be proud to own in full view?

dlb

3

Beyond the
Board

From age five to fifteen, I spent most weekday evenings in a taekwondo dojo. My Grand Master, Jong Park Soo, was a 9th Dan Black Belt from Korea, trained under General Choi Hong Hi, the founder of the International Taekwondo Federation (ITF). My personal instructor, Richard Parris, was a tall, commanding Bajan man—strong, disciplined, and formidable. Under his guidance, I learned more than martial arts; I learned discipline, resilience, and perhaps most importantly, how to see beyond the immediate.

To be honest, I can't say I loved martial arts as a child. I was overly sensitive—a self-proclaimed mama's boy who wasn't drawn to sports. My dad must have recognized himself in me because, in his own way, he was one too. I believe that's why he enrolled me in taekwondo—not to erase my sensitivity, but to fortify it. To teach me that strength isn't about brute force but about control, discipline, and focus. Looking back, I'm grateful.

The tenets of taekwondo—courtesy, integrity, perseverance, self-control, and indomitable spirit—became foundational. The lessons were both small and significant: maintaining eye contact to show respect, keeping my nails trimmed to prevent injury, delivering a firm handshake to project confidence. But beyond these, taekwondo taught me how to endure pain, overcome mental barriers, and most importantly, to rise after being knocked down.

One of the most profound lessons I learned came during a black belt test at age eleven. Unlike my previous belt tests, where I had trained out of obligation, this time I was fully prepared. I was doing this for myself, not for my father, not for my instructor—just for me.

The test began with patterns—fluid sequences that simulated defending against imaginary opponents. Then came sparring, where skill met strategy in controlled combat. I was ready for it all. But then, the board-breaking portion arrived.

There were two parts: first, a flying side kick over four crouching people to break a board with my foot. I soared through the air and landed the kick flawlessly.

Then came the second part—an open-hand strike meant to break a board held in place. That's where I hit a wall—literally and figuratively. Two failed attempts. My nerves got the best of me. Doubt crept in.

Then, one of my instructors leaned in and whispered, "You're focusing on the face of the board. Aim just beyond it."

That single shift in perspective changed everything. On my next attempt, the board snapped in two with ease.

That moment—one whisper, one shift—extended far beyond the dojo. So often in life, we fixate on our obstacles, allowing them to consume us. We see only the challenge in front of us and forget to aim beyond it—to the breakthrough waiting on the other side.

But aiming beyond the board? That wasn't just about seeing something different—it was about staying focused when everything in me wanted to quit. That's discipline. Discipline is what steadies your hands when nerves try to shake them. It's what pushes you to try again, not just because you can, but because you've trained yourself to.

In that moment, I didn't just shift my focus—I applied everything years of discipline had taught me: stay calm, trust your form, and strike with conviction. Focus and discipline aren't separate. They're partners. One helps you see the breakthrough. The other helps you reach it.

That small shift can have a monumental impact. When we focus beyond the challenge, we tap into a deeper well of strength, clarity, and purpose. We stop seeing obstacles as barriers and start seeing them as steps to something greater.

This isn't just about martial arts; it's about life. The principle of aiming beyond applies to every struggle we face. It's not about brute force. It's about focus.

Discipline was the force that carried me through those years of training, and it's one of the foundations of living a life of purpose. Discipline is what allows us to push past temporary discomfort and align our actions with our goals. Without it we will never see our breakthroughs.

I still remember the day I told my father I wanted to quit taekwondo. I admitted I'd only been doing it for him. His response was emphatic:

"You ain't doin' dis for me. You doin' dis for you."

I didn't fully get it then. But now, I see it clearly. My father was giving me a gift—an understanding that discipline isn't about obligation; it's about ownership. It's about taking responsibility for your own growth and pushing past perceived limitations. It's about showing up, even when you don't feel like it.

Mike Tyson once said, "Discipline is doing what you hate as if you love it." It's the driving force that turns vision into reality, that transforms dreams into tangible outcomes. Without it, we drift. With it, we soar.

Looking back, I see it now—discipline became one of my superpowers. It has shaped not just how I approach challenges, but how I approach life itself. And just like I learned to aim beyond the board, I've learned to consistently aim beyond obstacles—to set my sights on what lies ahead, not just what stands in my way.

What are you aiming for? Are you focused on the obstacle, or are you setting your sight beyond it? Take time to reflect. Do you need to develop greater discipline? Start with small habits that build over time. Discipline isn't about perfection; it's about persistence.

Discipline helps us endure through the current state. But at some point, we have to stop reacting and start designing. What if your life could be intentionally built?

Presumptuous in Practice

○ **Reflect:** Where in your life do you tend to lose focus when things get hard? Is it really the obstacle that's stopping you—or your ability to stay locked in?

✎ **Journal Prompt:** What breakthrough lies *just beyond* an area where you've been inconsistent?

▶ **Bold Move:** Choose one daily action you can repeat for the next 7 days that disciplines your focus—not just your effort.

☀ **Reframe:** Am I hitting the surface, or aiming through the barrier?

dlb

4

Design the
Outcome

¶‖P

I dreaded high school. Just the thought of navigating that massive building—packed with students who seemed to have it all together—was overwhelming. I wasn't just nervous—I was terrified. High school felt like a giant, and I was just a skinny kid standing in its shadow.

It wasn't just about fitting in. There were new classes, unfamiliar teachers, shifting social dynamics. And, for the first time, I had to take public transportation on my own. The idea of getting lost, missing my stop, or worse—drawing attention to myself—fed my anxiety. My fears were realized when, during my first week, a group of seniors cornered me at the back of the bus. As part of an initiation, they ordered me to do push-ups right there in the aisle. Humiliating. I felt smaller than ever, like I'd never find my footing in this new world.

But challenges have a way of hiding unexpected opportunities. High school wasn't just where I faced fear—it was where I discovered my strength. It was where I learned that I had the power to design my own outcome.

One of the most defining moments of that realization came during an event called M.O.G.A.—Most Outrageous Group Activity. It was a schoolwide competition filled with obstacle courses, relay races, and wild challenges. The grand prize was an all-expenses-paid trip to Canada's Wonderland, the massive theme park just outside of Toronto. For most, M.O.G.A. was just another fun event. But for me, it was an opportunity to take control—to create a moment that would redefine my high school experience.

At first glance, I wasn't the obvious choice to lead a team to victory. I wasn't an athlete. I wasn't popular. I was more comfortable moonwalking through the hallways than running relay races. But I had a vision. I decided I would build the best team our school had ever seen, and I wasn't going to let anything stand in my way.

The first step? Recruiting the right people. My friend Astor was the total package—smart, athletic, and well-respected. As student council president and future valedictorian, he set the tone for the type of team I wanted to assemble. His twin sister, a track star, was next. From there, I recruited her athletic friends. With each new addition, the vision became more real. With every new ask, I made sure they saw the conviction in my eyes. I wasn't just forming a team—I was creating something extraordinary. My belief in what we could achieve became contagious.

We named ourselves "American Gladiators," inspired by the hit TV show. The name alone put a target on our backs. We had to back up our talk with results, and that pressure only fueled our drive.

When event day arrived, we were ready. Obstacle courses, relay races, endurance tests—we attacked every challenge with locked-in focus and full-out drive. By the finals, we weren't just competing—we were dominating. And when the dust settled, we stood victorious, earning our trip to Canada's Wonderland.

The easy route would have been to join an existing team or stick to my immediate circle of friends. But I chose to aim higher. That experience taught me something I'd carry forever: when you have a clear vision and the conviction to chase it, you can design your outcome.

This lesson isn't just about winning a school competition.

It's about understanding that we have the power—the God-given ability—to shape our lives. Just as God spoke the world into existence, we, too, have the capacity to declare our outcomes into reality. When we decide, commit, and walk toward our goal, we activate a force that propels us forward into winning.

Think about that for a moment. Your words hold power. When you speak your goals out loud, you're not just making a statement—you're aligning your mind, body, and spirit with the future you're stepping into. Those words become a declaration, a commitment—not just to yourself, but to God, to your purpose, and to the divine path laid out for you.

And once you've made that declaration, something shifts. You begin to move with intention. You make choices that align with your vision. You start seeing doors open that you never noticed before. But here's the key—your goals and outcomes must align with your purpose. This isn't about wishful thinking or chasing after empty desires. It's about tapping into the deepest parts of your being and recognizing the calling God has placed on your life. When vision, words, and purpose align—momentum becomes inevitable. The universe itself begins to conspire in your favor, creating opportunities where there were once only obstacles.

Design the Outcome

So ask yourself: Are you actively designing the outcomes in your life, or are you letting life happen to you? Are your choices intentional, aligned with your purpose, or are you simply drifting, hoping that things will fall into place?

The story of M.O.G.A is more than a high school memory. It's proof that when you dare to believe in yourself—when you see beyond your circumstances and speak your truth—you set things in motion. You don't just reach goals; you create pathways for transformation, not only for yourself but for those around you.

Living a presumptuous life isn't just about chasing dreams— it's about designing them, shaping them, and bringing them to life. It's about speaking your vision with boldness, aligning it with your purpose, and then stepping forward in faith.

So, take control. Speak life into your dreams. Move with intention. Design your outcome. You're not just reacting to life. You're building it, one choice at a time. The outcomes you desire begin with the outcomes you decide.

Now, you can design an outcome, but that doesn't mean you're ready to be seen in it. Sometimes the real battle is not the doing—but the daring to be seen.

Presumptuous in Practice

○ **Reflect:** Write out one area of your life where you've been reactive.

✍ **Journal Prompt:** Declare (in writing) what outcome you really want.

▶▶ **Bold Move:** Craft 3 intentional choices that align with that outcome.

💡 **Reframe:** If I'm the architect, what blueprint am I designing?

dib

5
—
Hiding from Fame

¶¶

know a lot of people who are hiding. They show up to work, go through the motions, do just enough to get by— but something's missing. It's like they're afraid to be truly seen—to step fully into their gifts and share them with the world. Instead, they play it safe, keeping their light dimmed, staying in the background. Not because they don't know they have something special, but because they're afraid of what stepping out might mean. It's as if they're hiding from fame—not in the celebrity sense, but from the recognition that comes with owning their greatness.

I get it. I've been there.

On the surface, I was outgoing—the life of the party. But underneath, I was wrestling with insecurity. I remember a parent-teacher interview in primary school where my teacher told my parents I needed to raise my hand more, to share my thoughts and participate. My parents asked me why I wasn't speaking up, and I shrugged it off, but deep down, I knew the reason. I hated the sound of my own voice. I thought it was too high-pitched, sounded too much like a girl, and I was afraid of being mocked. So, I stayed silent. I kept my brilliance locked away and let fear dictate how I showed up in the world.

Then Michael Jackson changed everything. In my later elementary years, I became obsessed with his music, his performances, his presence. Something about him made me realize that uniqueness wasn't something to hide—it was something to celebrate. By grades seven and eight, I was doing Michael Jackson impersonations at talent shows, dancing and lip-syncing with confidence. For the first time, I felt free—unafraid to shine. I realized my gifts weren't just for me—they were meant to be shared, to spark joy, to inspire.

That stage gave me more than applause—it gave me joy. Pure, unfiltered joy. It reminded me that joy isn't just the reward for living boldly—it's the fuel that sustains it. When you feel that deep gladness bubbling up inside you while doing what you were made for? That's not coincidence. That's confirmation.

But then came high school, and I shrank back again. Maybe

it was the sting of being hazed as a scrawny ninth grader. Maybe it was the fear of standing out in a way that could make me a target. Whatever the reason, I told myself I'd never perform on a high school stage. I still entertained my peers in the hallways, moonwalking between classes, and my friends knew me as MJ. But the stage? That felt like too much.

Then, in grade twelve, everything changed.

The school was putting on a production of Fame, but they'd lost their lead, Leroy. That's when Mr. McDonald, a teacher who had seen my MJ impressions, started pursuing me for the role. He saw something in me that I was too afraid to see in myself. Every day, he showed up at my classes, reminding me that I was the perfect fit. He wouldn't let up. And finally, I said yes.

That yes changed everything. It was small in sound, but massive in impact.

The production became one of the most attended and successful musicals in the school's history. Our Fame cast photo and plaque were displayed alongside the athletic achievements—a historic moment for the dramatic arts. And for me, it was a personal breakthrough. I had spent years running from my own greatness, afraid of what it would mean to fully step into it. But when I finally did, I realized something profound: sometimes, we need a push. Sometimes, the nudge from someone else is the confirmation we need to step into the thing we already feel inside.

But this chapter isn't just about me. It's about you.

It's about recognizing that you can't hide from who you are. You can't keep playing small, hoping no one notices your brilliance. You were made for more, and the world needs what you carry. Living a presumptuous life means believing in your own greatness—not in arrogance, but in confidence. It's about knowing that your unique perspective, your gifts, your voice, and your presence have the power to make an impact.

So don't despise the nudges. The teachers, mentors, and friends who see something in you and refuse to let you hide—they're gifts. They're helping you see what you've been too afraid to acknowledge. And when you finally embrace it, everything changes.

Stop hiding. Stop doubting. Stop comparing.

You have every right to step boldly and joyfully into your calling. Even if you've hesitated in the past, even if you've let opportunities slip by, it's not too late to say yes. It's not too late to share what's inside of you with the world.

Think about Adam in the Garden of Eden. After eating the forbidden fruit, he hid from God, ashamed. And when God asked, *Who told you that you were naked?* He wasn't just asking about Adam's physical state—He was challenging the lie Adam had believed about himself.

Who told you that you're not enough? Who told you that you don't have what it takes? Who told you that your gifts don't matter? Who told you that you don't deserve joy?

I want you to reject those lies. You are worthy. You are loved. You have something to offer that no one else can. The world is waiting for the joy only you can bring.

Presumptuous means owning the fullness of who you are with faith in your steps, joy in your spirit, and boldness in your voice. It's about knowing that your gifts were never meant to be hidden. When you stop playing small and start living boldly, you unlock a life of purpose and fulfillment. And the most beautiful part? You won't just change your own life—you'll transform the lives of those around you.

The voice that shouts, '*You're not enough!*' is lying. And the voice that says, '*You're ready*'—even if it whispers—deserves a chance to be heard.

Once we stop hiding, we can begin listening. That inner voice, the divine nudge—it's been there all along. The question is: Will you trust it now?

dlb

Presumptuous in Practice

Reflect: Name a gift or talent you've been down-playing.

Journal Prompt: Journal about the first time you felt afraid to be seen.

Bold Move: Share your gift with someone this week— no fanfare, just presence.

Reframe: Ask: Who told me to hide, and why am I still listening?

6

—

You Already Know

¶‖₱

Fear has a way of paralyzing us—especially when it comes to taking that first step into the unknown. But here's the thing—that very first step sets everything else in motion. It's the foundation on which our dreams are built. Without action, we remain stagnant, stuck in place, unable to move forward.

Taking that first step isn't just about motion; it's about gaining insight. It's about learning how to navigate the obstacles ahead, making adjustments as we go, and discovering the possibilities that only reveal themselves when we decide to move. The simple act of moving forward opens doors we didn't even know were there.

Never underestimate the power of a small, sincere first step. It might seem insignificant at the time, but it is the catalyst for transformation.

The Unexpected Nudge

I'll never forget when I was seventeen, hanging out at the mall—something my dad wasn't thrilled about. He couldn't understand why I would spend time wandering through stores when I had no money to spend. Now, as a parent myself, I get it.

That day, while aimlessly strolling the mall, I came across a kiosk for Barbizon—a modeling school. The idea intrigued me. A school that taught people how to become models and actors? That sounded pretty cool.

If you've ever heard of Barbizon, you know it's often labeled a money-making scheme, preying on young hopefuls. But at that point in my life, I was really into acting. I had done a few school plays and felt a strong pull toward performing. My drama teacher had boosted my confidence, helping me believe I had what it took to succeed in the industry. So when I saw that kiosk, something inside me whispered, *this is part of your bigger picture.*

I took the brochures home and convinced my parents that this was something I wanted to pursue. I had been working for a few years and had saved up some money, so I told them I would pay for it myself. Reluctantly, they agreed, and my dad took me to the office to sign up.

During the process, they asked me to prepare a monologue and perform it for an associate. After my performance, the associate quickly stood up and said, "I've got to call someone to watch you do that again." They rushed out to get the owner of the company. Whether this was just part of their sales pitch or not, I'd already decided—this was a stepping stone to something greater.

For months, I attended Saturday workshops. I learned runway walking, posing for the camera, applying makeup, and even acting for commercials. Then one Saturday, our modeling coach announced an opportunity to attend an international modeling and talent competition in Los Angeles. It was likely another money-grabbing venture for the company, but I saw it as my next step. I convinced my parents, and once again, they supported me.

The competition brought months of training to a head. I placed in the top ten for Talent of the Year and performed in front of casting directors and agents. I felt one step closer. Then, my coach pulled me aside. An acting school in New York had seen my performance and wanted me to attend. They said my competition performance could serve as my audition.

There it was—the opportunity I had been waiting for.

But my dad had other hopes for me. He wanted me to become a lawyer or an architect—stable, "prestigious" careers. At the time, those options seemed reasonable, but looking back, I realize they were selections from the typical "successful career" hat. Society often pushes us toward choices without guiding us to discover what truly resonates within us.

For me, acting was it. Entertaining people, making them laugh, making them feel—that was my passion. It fueled me. That year, I graduated with the Dramatic Arts Award and returned for grade thirteen, knowing that I would be heading to New York the following year. The anticipation carried me through, filling me with purpose and joy.

Trusting the Inside Voice

When I saw that kiosk in the mall, I caught a glimpse of my future, and I heard my inner voice—even though it was just a *whisper*.

Most people experience moments like this and brush them off. Instead of leaning in, they quickly find reasons to dismiss the moment. They let distraction and doubt overshadow possibility.

But living a presumptuous life means paying attention to the stirring inside you that ignites the spark when something matters. We've become so conditioned to doubt ourselves that we've forgotten how to perceive it. We let the voices of so-called "realists" dull our senses and talk us into settling.

Here's the truth: that feeling deep in your gut—the one that excites and scares you—is real. It's pointing you toward your purpose. If you nurture it, discipline it, and act on it—it will lead you exactly where you're meant to be.

Most people never take the time to acknowledge their inner voice, let alone test its validity. They dismiss it as impractical or unrealistic. But when you start practicing the habit of listening and acting on those nudges, you build a mental muscle that helps you discern real direction. Over time, this becomes an intuitive skill—a guide you can trust in every decision.

Walking on Water

There's a story in the Bible that perfectly captures the power of stepping into the unknown. It's the story of Peter walking on water.

One night, Jesus told his disciples to go ahead of him in a boat while he stayed back to pray. Later, as the boat drifted in the middle of the sea, Jesus walked out to meet them—on the water. The disciples were terrified, thinking they had seen a ghost. But Jesus reassured them, saying, "Take courage, it is I; don't be afraid."

Peter, sensing something stir inside him, responded, "Lord, if it's you, tell me to come to you on the water." And Jesus simply said, "Come."

So Peter stepped out of the boat—and walked on water.

The lesson here isn't only about faith. It's about listening to the voice that calls you toward something greater— even something 'impossible'. It's about recognizing when an opportunity is presenting itself and having the courage to take the step, even when it feels uncertain.

Dare to Believe

I'm not here to tell you what to do, but I want to encourage you to tune in to that voice inside you—the one that's been nudging you, maybe even shouting at you, to take action. It's easy to get caught up in doubt, to talk yourself out of taking risks. But what if that voice is leading you exactly where you need to go?

Living a presumptuous life means daring to believe in that voice. It means trusting that your instincts are pointing you in the right direction, even when the path isn't fully clear.

Whatever it is that's calling you—a career shift, a creative pursuit, a personal goal, a relationship—listen.
Take that step. Trust that you won't sink.

That day at the Barbizon kiosk could've passed me by. But I listened. And that one small step toward my own voice reshaped everything.

There's a voice inside you that's been trying to speak for years. It's not loud—but it's steady. It won't push, but it also won't leave.

It's the voice that tells you when you've outgrown a version of yourself. The one that nudges you toward rooms you're afraid to walk into. The one that whispers truth even when no one else is saying it.

You already know. You've always known.

The question is—will you listen now?

Acting on what you know is brave. But becoming someone new in the process? That's the deeper work. Let's talk about being made.

Presumptuous in Practice

○ **Reflect:** Reflect on a time your gut nudged you—and you ignored it.

✍ **Journal Prompt:** What dream or idea have you already known, but not acted on?

▶ **Bold Move:** Take the tiniest step in that direction today.

💡 **Reframe:** What would trusting myself look like in motion?

dlb

7

Making It vs. Being Made

¶ℙ

As my last year of high school wound down, I found myself wrestling with uncertainty. The initial excitement of moving to New York to study acting was slowly being replaced by doubt. Reality began to sink in—how would I pay for everything? Where would I live? Who did I know there? And all that unknown? It was overwhelming.

My mom, a natural worrier, only amplified my anxiety. She reminded me of every possible danger, every challenge of living in a big city, especially one as intense as New York. Her concerns, though well-intended, made me question whether I was making the right decision.

At that point in my life, my faith wasn't as strong as it is now, but I still believed in the power of prayer. So, I asked God for a clear sign. If New York was where I was meant to be, I needed Him to confirm it. And when you ask with a sincere heart, God has a way of answering in ways you can't ignore.

There was a required administration fee to secure my spot at the school before tuition payments were due. It was an oddly specific amount—$129.32. I had the money, but in that moment, I was looking for a divine confirmation that this was the right path.

A few months prior, I had done a modeling gig for a hair brand called American Crew. Why they booked me, I'll never know—my hair definitely didn't match their product lineup. But it was a job my agency arranged, and I had completely forgotten about it. Out of the blue, a check arrived in the mail. The amount? Exactly $129.32.

Some might dismiss that as coincidence, but when you're paying attention, you recognize life's subtle whispers. That check was my sign. With renewed confidence, I finalized my paperwork and prepared to step into the unknown.

The Journey Begins

With my tuition secured, the next challenges were finding a place to live and knowing someone in the city. Fortunately, a friend from my agency, Anthony Clarke, had also been accepted to the school and was considering attending. Anthony was like the chocolate Hulk—British accent,

Jamaican slang, hip-hop swagger. Talented, hilarious, and charismatic, he was someone I admired. After talking, we decided to become roommates, referring to each other as "cousins," in that easy, familiar way close friends do. We were ready to take over the world together.

The next step was finding a place to stay. Our agency informed us that our acting coach would also be teaching at the school. Without hesitation, we asked if we could crash with him until we found our own place. He agreed. It seemed like everything was falling into place.

But when we arrived, we realized the situation wasn't as straightforward as we'd hoped. Our coach was actually subletting a room in someone else's apartment, and he was out of town. The main tenant, clearly unimpressed with our presence, tolerated us but made it clear we weren't exactly welcome. Despite the discomfort, we were grateful. It wasn't ideal, but it was enough. We had a roof—and a reason to begin.

The City That Shapes You

Leaving my suburban comfort zone to live in New York was terrifying. But divine confirmation had given me the courage to push past my fears. I came to New York thinking I needed to "make it." But God was more interested in making me—

shaping me through challenges, hardships, and experiences I never could have anticipated. Success wasn't just about reaching a destination; it was about becoming the kind of person who could handle the journey.

That reality became even clearer when I was part of a singing trio in New York. None of us could really sing, but we were determined to "make it." We practiced, wrote songs, and tried (and mostly failed) to harmonize. Yet, in our audacity, we decided we were ready for Amateur Night at the Apollo.

If you know anything about the Apollo Theater, you know it's not for the faint of heart. The audience doesn't just watch—you either impress them, or they'll boo you off the stage. Many legendary artists have been humbled by those unforgiving Harlem crowds, including a young Lauryn Hill.

Predictably, our group's audition was a disaster. We didn't make the cut. Deflated, we walked away from the theater, knowing we had lost an opportunity.

But something in me wouldn't let it go. Before we boarded the subway home, I turned to my group and said, "Would you mind if I went back and auditioned alone?" They hesitated, but ultimately agreed.

I ran back to the theater, contemplating what song to sing. I settled on April Showers by Dru Hill. Despite not being a trained singer, I knew I could perform. And sometimes, confidence is enough.

I walked into the audition room and asked if I could try again—this time solo. They looked at me skeptically but allowed it.

I sang with everything I had:

> *Loving you is all I need. Never take your love from me, 'cause I think I would lose my mind if you would go away...*

To my surprise, they liked it. I was invited to perform at Amateur Night.

Standing backstage that night, I touched the famous Tree of Hope stump—the same one countless legends before me had touched. Even Michael Jackson. I wasn't just about to perform; I was stepping into history.

When I started singing, I could hear uncertainty in my voice—and in the audience's murmurs. A few boos erupted from the left side. I didn't panic. Instead, I turned and sang directly to them, winning them over. Then I did the same with the right side. By the end, I wasn't booed off the stage. I didn't win either. But I walked away with something far more valuable: an understanding of human nature and the power of my own presence.

The Making Process

Fear convinces us of a future failure that hasn't even happened. Had I let fear control me, I never would have returned to that theater. But I learned that I had the ability to influence an outcome through my own actions. Instead of shrinking under pressure, I stepped into it. And that choice changed the outcome.

This experience reinforced a deep truth. Many of us let fear, doubt, or external circumstances dictate our lives. We convince ourselves that we don't have enough talent, resources, connections, or knowledge to move forward. But more often than not, those limitations are self-imposed.

What I learned in New York is that "making it" isn't about achieving external success—it's about being made through the journey. Every hardship, every challenge, every uncomfortable moment was shaping me into the person I was meant to be.

Your Journey

If you're in a season of uncertainty, feeling like you haven't "made it" yet, I want you to shift your perspective. The obstacles in front of you aren't roadblocks; they're stepping stones. They are refining you, preparing you for what's ahead.

We get so fixated on the destination, we forget the journey is where the shaping happens. God isn't just leading you to a place—He's shaping you into the person who can thrive once you get there.

So if you feel stuck, if doors aren't opening as fast as you'd like, or if challenges keep coming, trust the process. You're not just trying to make it. You're being made.

Keep moving forward. Keep stretching beyond your comfort zone. Keep believing that what's ahead is worth every struggle. Because it is.

And your ability to consistently believe, both in yourself and in what's ahead of you? That's where faith begins.

Presumptuous in Practice

○ **Reflect:** Write down 3 ways you've grown in the last 5 years.

✍ **Journal Prompt:** Where do you feel shaped by the journey, not just the result?

▶▶ **Bold Move:** Celebrate one area of progress, not outcome.

💡 **Reframe:** Ask: What is this season making me into—not just leading me to?

dIb

8

Found by Faith

Faith can be a touchy subject—I get that. I'm not a fan of religion in the traditional sense either. There's a big difference between following religious rules and having a genuine relationship with Jesus. Religion, as most people know it, gets tangled in rituals, traditions, and expectations. But faith? Faith is something different. It's deeply personal, transformative, and powerful.

Regardless of your personal beliefs, I hope you'll lean into my experience and see the value in the perspective I'm sharing. This isn't about pushing beliefs on anyone—it's about how faith shaped my journey and gave me the courage to live a bold, purpose-driven life.

Faith is the cornerstone of a presumptuous life. It's the doorway that lets us step into the unknown—to believe in what we can't yet see, and to trust that our lives are part of a greater plan. It gives us strength when we feel weak, direction when we feel lost, and hope when things don't go as expected. For me, faith in Jesus became my foundation—the thing that gave me confidence in the unseen and resilience in the face of challenges. But my faith wasn't always strong. It had to be found.

Losing My Way

New York was everything I imagined it would be—electric, exhilarating, full of opportunity. But it also tested me in ways I didn't expect. After a year and a half at acting school, I made the difficult decision to drop out. Not because I couldn't handle the work, but because I started to feel like the program was designed to churn out actors in a specific mold.

Everyone was being shaped into the same style, the same cadence, the same approach. It didn't sit right. I wanted to be me, to bring something unique to the table. The school wanted to fit me into their mold, but I had a sense that God had a different blueprint for me. I was realizing that there's a difference between being made into something by man, and being shaped into who you are by God.

Dropping out left me feeling unmoored. I was working retail at HMV in Herald Square, trying to figure out what was next. I felt lost, insecure, and more uncertain about my future than ever. I had a girlfriend at the time, but even that relation-ship didn't provide the clarity or stability I was searching for. Looking back, I now recognize that I was slipping into depression. It wasn't something I had the language for at the time, but I knew something wasn't right.

When I felt low, I turned to what my parents had always encouraged—prayer and the Bible. It wasn't like I had a deep spiritual life back then, but in my search for answers, I picked up my Bible almost every day. Eventually, I read through the entire New Testament—page by page, searching for something I couldn't yet name.

I was raised Catholic. Church wasn't foreign to me, but I had never been exposed to the idea of a personal relationship with God. I prayed, but I didn't yet know what it meant to connect with God. I was searching for answers externally when what I really needed was an internal transformation.

At 20 years old, I hit a breaking point. I wanted to go home. I wanted to retreat to my parents' house, to my old bed, to the familiarity of that space. I told my girlfriend how I felt, and it hurt her. She wanted to be enough to keep me there—but deep down, I knew she couldn't be.

I booked a trip home, not knowing if I'd return to New

York. Looking back, I should have recognized it for what it was—God was already pulling me in a different direction.

The Detour That Changed Everything

After spending time at home, I packed up and got ready for the long Greyhound bus ride back to New York. The trip to the border was uneventful. When I got to U.S. customs, I approached the officer and stated my reason for entry.

I said I was still in school.

The reality? I wasn't. And my visa, which allowed me to work, was only valid if I remained in school.

For some strange reason, the officer asked to see my wallet. Inside, I had a pay stub from my job and a picture of my girlfriend. Whether it was meant to be or just a coincidence, the officer denied me entry. Just like that, my New York chapter closed.

At the time, it felt like failure. I had to break up with my girlfriend. I had to ask my roommate to bring my stuff back in trips. I lay in my old bed, staring at the ceiling, wondering how I got here.

But looking back, it was one of the best things that ever happened to me.

The Path to Faith

Two things happened that shifted everything.

First, my dad became my biggest encourager. Almost every day, he'd come into my room, give me a fist bump, and tell me everything was going to be all right. He reminded me that my path didn't have to look like everyone else's and that I shouldn't compare myself to others. His words were a lifeline.

The second thing was an invitation. A friend invited me to visit a youth group at her church. I'd never been to a born-again, non-denominational, Pentecostal church before. But my friend was a pretty girl, and I figured, why not?

I walked in expecting to feel out of place. But what I found was surprising. The church was full of people my age, excited to be there. They had a youth choir that sounded incredible. It wasn't stiff or boring—it felt alive. And when the pastor started preaching, I actually listened.

Then something unexpected happened. At the end of the service, the pastor called me out and said, "Do *you know that you are called to impact generations?*"

It was the strangest thing. It felt like he was speaking directly to something buried deep inside me. Without thinking, I responded, "Yes, I do."

February 29, 2000—a leap year. That was the day I gave my life to the Lord.

Letting Go to Be Found

Faith isn't about having all the answers. It's about trusting that even when things fall apart, God is still in control.

For me, faith became an anchor. I started attending church, surrounding myself with people who encouraged me, and letting go of relationships that weren't aligned with where I was headed. It wasn't about perfection. It was about surrender. I had to surrender to a process and allow myself to be shaped by something bigger than me.

A few months in, the church announced a baptism. I hesitated. I thought I needed to reach a certain level of spirituality before I was "ready." But a friend named Maxine set me straight. "That's not how it works," she said.

Baptism isn't about arriving at perfection. It's an outward declaration of an inward decision. It's saying, I choose this path.

I did it. And in doing so, I sealed my decision to trust that God had a better plan for my life than the one I was desperately trying to build on my own.

The Journey Forward

Sometimes, we have to lose our life in order to find it. I thought I was giving up on my dream. But I was making room for something greater.

Faith means believing that the detours are part of the plan. It means trusting that even when things don't go the way we expect, we are exactly where we need to be. If you're holding on too tightly to your own plans, afraid to let go, I encourage you—trust the process. The life you're meant to live might just be on the other side of the life you're afraid to lose.

Faith isn't about certainty. It's about taking the next step, even when you can't see the full path. And when you do, you'll find that every detour, every setback, and every unexpected turn was leading you somewhere greater all along.
And that's how it happened for me.

I didn't go searching for faith with all the right answers.
I didn't earn it or figure it all out first.
I just kept walking.

And in the middle of the detours, doubt, and broken plans...

I was found—found by faith.

Faith doesn't need qualifications. God doesn't ask for our resume. But we still measure ourselves by the standards of men and their credentials. Maybe it's time to challenge the paper trail.

Presumptuous in Practice

💡 **Reflect:** Map your spiritual turning points—no matter how small.

✍🏻 **Journal Prompt:** Write a letter to God from where you are today.

▶ **Bold Move:** Say yes to something faith-filled this week.

💡 **Reframe:** Am I trusting a path I design, or one I discern?

dlb

9

It's More Than What's on Paper

¶P

When I got back from New York, I needed a job. So, like most people, I hit the mall and started handing out applications. I ended up working at Spencer Gifts, a novelty shop, for a few months until a friend from church told me about an opening at his workplace, *Moores Clothing for Men.* If you're not familiar, it's a men's suit store—sharp suits, polished shoes, everything you need to look your best. Up to that point, the only times I'd ever worn a suit were for my First Communion and my Grade 8 Confirmation ceremonies. But a job is a job, and *Moores* felt like a step up from a novelty shop, so I decided to give it a shot. I met with the manager, and before I knew it, I was hired as a clothing associate.

My job was straightforward: help put together looks for the wardrobe consultant whenever clients came in. I'd find the right ties, pocket squares, shirts, and accessories to complement the suit they were selecting. It wasn't bad. I got to dress up in a suit every day, the atmosphere was laid-back, and the staff was easy to get along with.

Into the Unknown

A few months into the job, a notice came in about an opening at the head office. They were looking for a property manager assistant. This was a big deal—*Moores* had 114 stores across Canada and a few in the U.S., and this role oversaw everything from building maintenance to utilities, rent negotiations, sign repairs, snow and garbage removal, and more. It was a serious step up from selling suits.

I remember thinking, *Maybe I should apply.* But when I mentioned it to a coworker, his reaction was almost dismissive, like I had overstepped some unspoken boundary. He laughed it off, saying, "You can't do that."

It wasn't just the words—it was the tone. The unspoken message: Know your place. Stay in your lane. Don't aim too high. That job isn't for people like you.

That kind of comment can either shrink you or fuel you. For me, it lit a fire. I figured, *why not?* Just because he thinks I can't doesn't mean I shouldn't try. His doubt became my motivation. I applied for the job, even though I had no experience in property management. I knew I'd be stepping into unfamiliar territory, but I also knew that learning on the job is sometimes the best way to grow.

People Will Project Their Own Limits on You

Sometimes, people project their own insecurities onto you. Maybe they don't believe in their own ability to take risks, so they assume you shouldn't either. It's easy to absorb that doubt, to let it seep into your own thinking. But here's the choice you need to make: Are you going to accept their limitations as your own? Or are you going to push past them and see what you're really capable of?

I chose to push past. I refused to let someone else's narrow view of what was possible dictate my actions. I knew the only way to find out if I could do it was to take the chance.

I sent off an email expressing my interest and managed to set up an interview. The interview was with Dennis Button, VP of Store Development. It turned out to be one of the best interviews I've ever had. We talked about the job for maybe fifteen minutes—and music for over an hour. Dennis was a fellow music lover. We talked about everything from Michael Jackson and Motown to Tower of Power, Earth, Wind & Fire, Kool & the Gang, and Stevie Wonder.

At the end of that hour-and-a-half interview, Dennis offered me the job. He said something that stuck with me: "I know you won't stay here for long, but I'll enjoy the time while I have you."

His words hit differently. He saw something in me—something beyond the role I was applying for. It wasn't just about offering me the job; it was about recognizing my potential. That realization was empowering. I may not have had the experience on paper, but I had something that can't be measured by a resume: the willingness to step up, take a shot at something bigger, and grow into the person he believed I could become.

The Power of Being Seen

Over the next year, I learned a lot—not just about property management, but about business, leadership, and, of course, music. Dennis took me under his wing in a way that went beyond the typical boss-employee relationship. He didn't just assign tasks; he invited me into high-level meetings, asked for my input, and gave me space to grow and learn. He treated me not just as an assistant, but as someone with something valuable to contribute.

The mentorship I received from Dennis wasn't just about business. He taught me how to lead with integrity and build relationships that last. He nurtured what he saw in me and helped shape my journey in ways I'm still grateful for today.

Our relationship grew into a real friendship, one that lasted long after I moved on from *Moores*. Years later, I had the honor of officiating his daughter's wedding—a testament to the kind of bond we built.

It's More Than What's on Paper

This experience taught me that what qualifies you isn't always what's on paper. Sometimes, what qualifies you is simply your willingness to say yes to opportunities, even when others doubt your readiness. If I had listened to my coworker or waited until I *felt* qualified, I would have missed out on an experience that set the stage for so much more in my life.

But here's the thing: sometimes, the people who doubt you the most are the ones closest to you—parents, friends, coworkers. They may not mean to hold you back, but they're projecting their own fears and insecurities onto you. They might be thinking practically, looking at what's on paper, and based on that, they might be right. But they're not looking at what's inside. They don't see the full scope of your potential.

This is where your faith and intuition come in. You have to

trust that deeper sense of knowing that says you're made for more. Because the truth is, your qualifications don't just come from your resume; they come from your calling. They come from God, who has equipped you with everything you need to fulfill your purpose.

Are there areas where you've held back because someone else didn't think you were ready? Have you let someone else's limitations become your own? If so, it's time to shift your mindset.

The next time an opportunity presents itself, don't hesitate because you don't feel fully qualified. Trust that you'll rise to the occasion—even if you don't feel ready yet. The most important qualifications—the ones that truly make a difference—aren't the ones listed on paper. They're the ones that come from within: courage, boldness, and the willingness to step into the unknown.

Dennis saw in me what paper couldn't prove.

Sometimes, someone else's belief in you shows up at just the right time to confirm what you only dared to hope.

What happens when someone believes in you before the world does? Hopefully, you'll pay it forward—and start creating space for someone else to grow. That's what comes next.

Presumptuous in Practice

💡 **Reflect:** List the ways you've undervalued yourself.

✍️ **Journal Prompt:** Journal what makes you qualified beyond your resume.

▶▶ **Bold Move:** Apply for or ask for something you don't feel ready for.

💡 **Reframe:** Who said you needed a stamp to be significant?

dlb

10

The J.A.M!

¶|P

One random day in late February 2001, my pastor called me into her office. I wasn't sure what to expect. I racked my brain trying to remember if I'd done anything to warrant a serious talk—but came up with nothing. So, I walked in, curious and maybe a little bit anxious. As soon as I sat down, she cut right to the chase. She'd been watching me—seeing my background in the arts and how I was getting more involved with the youth ministry. She saw something in me—a passion for using the arts to connect with young people—and she wanted to encourage that.

She wanted me to start a monthly event for the youth— something creative, engaging, and full of life. She gave me the freedom to build it however I wanted, with one condition: it had to be called *The J.A.M!*

The idea immediately got me excited. I knew exactly what I wanted *The J.A.M!* to be—a space where young people could showcase their talents, connect with each other, and experience something that was both entertaining and meaningful. My mind was racing with possibilities. This wasn't just another event; it was an opportunity to create a platform that combined my love for the arts with a deeper purpose. The more I thought about it, the more I realized that this could be something special, something that would resonate far beyond just a monthly gathering. It felt like the pieces of my life were coming together in a way that made sense, aligning with a path I couldn't see this clearly before.

Now, what most people don't know—and what I never actually said on stage—is that J.A.M. stood for Jesus and Me.

Yeah. I know.

Even back then, I thought it was... a little cheesy. What our kids today would call *cringe*.

But listen—if you're from the city and you came to *The J.A.M!* I guarantee you didn't know that's what it meant. Because I don't think I ever said it out loud. I just rolled with *The J.A.M!* and let the branding carry us.

And it *worked*.

The J.A.M! felt like a mashup of Saturday Night Live and In Living Color. We had comedy sketches, musical guests, and an open mic segment that brought out some of the best talent in the city. Youth from different church groups and communities would gather each month, drawn by the energy and excitement of the event. But it wasn't just about the performances—it was the atmosphere—a place where creativity and faith intersected, where young people could express themselves freely and authentically.

One of the segments we created was called *"Conversations with God."* It was a lighthearted, comedic bit where I'd bring up humorous thoughts or questions to God—things that would make the audience laugh but also think. It was meant to be fun, but it had a deeper layer to it. It was a subtle reminder that talking to God doesn't always have to be serious or formal; it could be casual, like an ongoing conversation with a friend.

The Promise of Something Greater

The J.A.M! quickly became a blueprint of my journey, a place where the bigger picture of what God was doing in my life started to come into focus. It was there that I met artists like Promise, who would become instrumental in shaping the next chapter of my story. Promise wasn't just another performer; he was someone whose talent and presence were undeniable. The first time I saw him on stage, I knew he was something special. If I were Berry Gordy from Motown, Promise was my Smokey Robinson. He had that rare mix of stage presence, lyrical depth, and wordplay—the kind that made you sit up and pay attention. I knew right away that I wanted to work with him.

As we began to collaborate, it became clear that Promise wasn't just another artist; he was the spark that would ignite a new phase in my life. Together, we worked on projects that allowed me to put into practice the things I had been dreaming about—developing artists and creating music that could reach people on a deeper level. *The J.A.M!* provided the outlet I needed to explore these ideas and bring them to life.

Building the Dream: S4 Entertainment

S4 Entertainment was born during this season—an artist management and event planning company I founded with the vision of "*Changing the way you live.*" My mission was to create a platform that would introduce art and artists to the world who could inspire, uplift, and provoke thought.

One of the shining examples of S4's impact was Roshana. I first met her at a youth retreat when she was just 13 years old. I heard her humming as she passed me by, and I knew she was a singer. I walked up and asked if she'd ever consider doing music. Her answer?

An uncomfortable but firm "absolutely not". I told her, "When you're ready, let me know." Two years later, after a Sunday service, Roshana came up to me at the sound booth and said, "I'm ready now." It was as if the two years since I asked her the question had been just a day.

We immediately sprang into action. I connected her with a young producer named Micah "Chozen" Williams, who was also 15 years old. I thought it would be amazing to have two 15-year-olds produce, record, and release their own album. For the next few months, we crisscrossed the city to Promise's home studio to write songs and produce an album for Roshana. The following year, we released her album, which was very well received. One of her singles, "*Steady*", even played on mainstream radio in Toronto and charted nationally on Christian music charts. Roshana and Promise's journeys are early examples of the presumptuous thinking and living I embraced from the start. She initially hesitated but eventually embraced her gift and pursued it with boldness and determination.

Through these experiences, S4 Entertainment became a training ground for audacious dreams and bold actions. The artists we nurtured and the events we organized all carried the spirit of presumptuous living.

We didn't wait for opportunities to come to us; we created them.

We didn't conform to the expectations of the world; we redefined them.

S4 influenced many artists who continue to make significant impacts both locally and globally, even today.

The Bigger Conversation

Living a presumptuous life is about staying in tune with the conversations God is having with you. It's about listening for His voice—in everyday moments, unexpected meetings, and even the lighthearted ones. Sometimes, the guidance you need comes in the most unexpected ways.

As you reflect on your own life, think about the conversations you've been having with God—whether through prayer, through others, or through those quiet moments in your heart. Are you listening? Are you staying open to the nudges that could be guiding you toward your next big step?

The J.A.M! taught me that hearing God's voice isn't always about grand revelations; sometimes, it's about the small, consistent conversations that lead you in the right direction. Keep the lines of communication open. You never know when God might drop a word or an idea that could change everything.

The J.A.M! taught me that building platforms is powerful—but sometimes, the biggest shifts don't happen on a stage. They happen in your personal life. That's where my next chapter begins—with someone I met through The J.A.M! who would end up changing everything.

Presumptuous in Practice

○ **Reflect:** Recall the last time you created something that served others.

✍ **Journal Prompt:** Design a space (physical or virtual) to uplift someone else's gift.

▶ **Bold Move:** Invite one person into that space this week.

💡 **Reframe:** Ask: Am I hoarding my platform or multiplying it?

dlb

11

Wait for Me

¶¶

There are moments in life when everything shifts—when you can literally feel the course of your journey realigning. Meeting Juli-Anne in 2002 was one of those moments. It felt like God Himself had rearranged time and space to bring our lives together. It wasn't something I saw coming, but when it happened, I knew deep down that my life was about to change in a way I couldn't quite put into words. From the moment we connected, I felt a pull, a deep sense of knowing that this woman was meant to be a part of my story—our lives were meant to intertwine in a way that would shape the rest of our days. And while our story could fill another book (and it probably will someday), the lesson I learned through our journey is one I need to share: If you don't know who you are or where you're headed, you can't recognize who's meant to go with you.

It all started with a mutual friend, Melissa, who had heard

Juli-Anne perform some of her spoken word pieces. Juli-Anne has a way with words, and our friend was captivated by the depth and passion in her poetry—so much so that she immediately thought of *The J.A.M!* She reached out to me and suggested I invite Juli-Anne to perform. To be honest, I didn't think much of it at first—it was just another performer, another talent to showcase. But that simple suggestion became something far more significant than I ever imagined. What began as a routine call to invite her to the event evolved into a deep, four-hour conversation that neither of us saw coming. By the time we hung up, I knew in my gut that I had just met my wife.

During that conversation, there was a moment that caught me completely off guard—a moment when I found myself saying something that felt both spontaneous and deeply significant. I asked her to wait for me. It was such a strange thing to say, especially since this was our first real conversation. But in that moment, I had this uncanny sense of clarity about our future together. It's a weird thing, seeing a glimpse of your future so vividly, only to be pulled back into the present, realizing that there's still a journey to walk through before that vision can become reality. That one line—*wait for me*—was my heart's way of acknowledging the weight of what I felt, even if my mind wasn't fully ready to grasp it. But as much as I could see where we were headed,

I also knew I had to go through the process of becoming the man I needed to be for that future to manifest.

As our conversation unfolded, it became clear that Juli-Anne and I connected on so many levels—our moral values, backgrounds, beliefs, and even our mindset and outlook on life seemed so aligned. We shared similar goals for the future, and it felt like we were on the same wavelength in ways that were both comforting and exhilarating. So, when I said, "wait for me", it wasn't just a smooth line or me trying to be slick; it was my heart recognizing something deeply significant in her, something that felt right on every level.

But as much as I felt that connection, there was also the reality of my immediate situation—I was already in a relationship with a girl that I had just started talking to a couple of weeks before. Deep down, I knew this relationship wasn't right for me, but for some reason, I chose to stay in it. It was as if I needed to prove to myself that she *wasn't* the one, almost like I was trying to justify the gut feeling that had already told me as much. It was a confusing time, where my heart was pulling me in one direction, while my choices were trying to hold me back in another. And so, even with this newfound connection with Juli-Anne, I found myself entangled in a situation that didn't serve me well. I was delaying the inevitable for reasons I didn't fully understand.

When I asked Juli-Anne to wait for me, I wasn't just asking her to wait for a future that I could already sense, but I was also acknowledging that I wasn't yet the person I needed to be for her. I knew deep down that I had some growing to do, that I had to shed the layers of who I was and evolve into the man who could truly walk beside her. At the time, I was stuck in a version of relationships I had seen all around me. The ones depicted in movies and sad R&B songs, full of toxic patterns, broken dynamics, and settling for less than what I knew I needed and deserved.

These skewed depictions had subtly crept in and become my standard, even though my heart was crying out for something more, something healthier, something real. And so, I found myself caught between the pull of what I knew was right with Juli-Anne and the grip of what I had subconsciously accepted as the norm.

Presumptuous means recognizing when you're living below the standard you know you're called to—and refusing to settle there. It demands the bravery to dig deep and pull out what's needed to grow into the version of you that's ready for greatness.

During those seven long years of waiting, I stayed in touch with Juli-Anne, but from a distance. She was always there, in the background of my life. She became the voice of reason I turned to whenever my mind was clouded. Whenever I needed clarity or a sense of calm, I found myself calling her. She had this incredible ability to bring me back to center, to remind me of who I was and what I was capable of.

Then came that pivotal night when I called her out of the blue, and she sensed that I was struggling. She invited me to meet for coffee, and it was there, in the quiet of that night, that I reconnected to me. As we talked, I told her something that had been stirring in me for a long time: "The version of me that I am with you is who I always want to be".

She brought out the best version of me—the man I was destined to be—the man I always knew I was.

As we sat in the parked car, with the light on, it was as if the light began to intensify, literally and figuratively, and I saw her in a way I had never seen before. "You're a pretty girl," I said. I was seeing her for the first time—even though I'd known her for years. We call that day Epiphany Day because it was then that I finally understood what my heart had been trying to tell me all along—Juli-Anne was the one.

Sometimes, you have to be willing to wait, to lock in, to do your work, and to allow yourself the time to mature. That way when the right moment comes, you don't miss it—you're ready to step into it fully and without hesitation.

Trusting your gut is an important part of this process. Your intuition is often the first nudge in the right direction, the whisper that tells you when something—or someone—is right for you. Don't waste time second-guessing yourself or waiting for things to become clearer. When you know something, act on it. The longer you wait, the more you risk delaying your destiny.

Are you the person you need to be to recognize and embrace the life and partnership you're meant to have? If not, start your work today. Don't leave your future partner, your friends, your children—even your purpose—waiting on the version of you you're still avoiding.

Because some relationships change everything. And some ideas do, too—if you're bold enough to go first. The next chapter is for the forerunners.

Presumptuous in Practice

💡   **Reflect:** Write a letter to the version of you someone's waiting for.

✍️   **Journal Prompt:** What habits or healing must you prioritize to become that version?

▶️   **Bold Move:** Make one commitment today toward that growth.

💡   **Reframe:** What if delay is development, not denial?

db

12

Forerunner

¶¶

Ideas are powerful. They begin as whispers—fleeting thoughts that are easy to ignore. But if nurtured—if acted on with faith and determination, they can shape our realities and create opportunities we never saw coming.

The challenge is that too many people dismiss their ideas before they even get the chance to breathe life into them. They doubt, they hesitate, they convince themselves that the idea is too small or insignificant to matter.

But here's the truth: ideas are seeds. They don't start as towering trees; they start as something small, something uncertain. The potential for greatness isn't in how big the idea seems at first—it's in your willingness to trust it, to believe that something unseen can grow into something real. It takes faith to act on an idea, to move forward without having all the details figured out. But when you take that first step, when you dare to believe in the unseen, doors begin to open in ways you never expected.

This chapter is about one of those moments in my life—when I had to stop waiting and go first. About how a simple idea—born out of frustration and a desire to create more opportunities for my artists—evolved into something far greater than I could have imagined. It's about what it means to be a forerunner: someone who builds what others are still waiting to find. It's about paving your own path when the road you need doesn't exist.

Born of Frustration

By this point, S4 Entertainment was making moves. We had built a reputation. The artists we were working with were talented and passionate, and things were steadily gaining momentum. Some were working on projects, others were performing locally, and a few were diving into songwriting and collaborating with newer talents.

But one thing gnawed at me: waiting.

Waiting for an artist to finish a project. Waiting for them to be ready to record. Waiting for them to book shows. Waiting for opportunities to present themselves. My momentum felt tied to other people—and that frustrated me. I hated the feeling of being stagnant, of sitting around with my hands tied, waiting for something to happen.

I wanted to build something that could move at my pace—something that would keep the momentum going, regardless of what was happening with any individual artist. And then, an idea hit me.

I had always loved magazines. There was something about flipping through a fresh, glossy issue filled with striking photography, compelling interviews, and bold visuals. I imagined my artists being featured in a magazine, seeing their stories and their talents celebrated in print. But they weren't famous. Getting them featured in a major, existing publication wasn't going to happen anytime soon.

So, I thought, why wait for someone else to feature them? Why not create my own magazine?

From a Thought to a Thing

The moment I decided to act on the idea, something shifted. It wasn't just about the magazine itself—it was about taking control of the narrative, about creating a platform instead of waiting for one.

I had a background in graphic design and was skilled with

Adobe software, so I started sketching a concept—laying out the pages, crafting a sleek, modern look, and placing mock articles featuring Promise—our standout artist—on the cover. We had just done an incredible photo shoot, so I sprinkled in a few other artists, added fake advertisements, and polished it until it looked like a real, professional publication.

This mock-up wasn't just a prototype; it was a vision in print. I imagined walking into barbershops and local restaurants, seeing people flipping through the pages, discovering the artists, reading about their music. I had no advertisers lined up yet, no distribution strategy—just the belief that if I could make this vision tangible, the rest would follow.

And that's when something unexpected happened.

Not Just a Call—A Catalyst

Before I could even start pitching to advertisers, I got a call from Tony Cooper, a well-respected figure in the Christian music industry. Tony had been making waves in Christian entertainment, breaking new ground in ways that were fresh, exciting, and innovative.

To this day, I still don't know how he heard about the magazine idea—but the fact that he did was a game-changer. Tony loved the concept and, without hesitation, pitched it to Christian Media Corporation (CMC), a major Christian music and entertainment distribution company in Canada.

They didn't just like it—they wanted in.

CMC came back with a proposal:
- They would print 20,000 copies of the magazine every other month.
- They would cover the printing costs.
- We would keep the advertising revenue.

This was massive.

To put it into perspective, a magazine typically operates with a 50/50 split between content and advertising. With 32 pages, that meant 16 ad pages—each selling for about $1,000 a page.

Do the math.

What started as a simple idea to give my artists a bit of exposure had suddenly turned into a nationally distributed magazine—one where we controlled the content, the creative direction, and the revenue.

That's the heart of a forerunner: someone who steps out in

faith so others can follow with confidence.

I didn't have a road to follow—I had to make one.

This wasn't something I could have orchestrated on my own.

This was God taking my small step of faith and multiplying it beyond what I could have imagined.

Inspired Magazine

With this opportunity locked in, Inspired Magazine was officially born. I became the co-editor-in-chief, writing news articles, reviewing music, and covering entertainment stories happening across Canada and the U.S.

We received free CDs every month to review, movie passes, and even got to present an award at the GMA Canada Covenant Awards—all because I decided to act on a simple idea.

What's crazy is that I had no qualifications to run a magazine.

I didn't have a journalism degree.

I didn't have industry connections.

I had no blueprint. No model for how this was supposed to work.

But what I did have was belief. I had faith that if I stepped out, if I took what was in my hands and did something with it, God would take care of the rest. And that's exactly what happened. This experience reinforced a powerful truth: it doesn't matter where you start, only that you start.

Had I dismissed the magazine idea as too small or unrealistic, I never would have known what was possible. I never would have landed national distribution. I never would have gotten my foot in the door of the media industry.

What ideas have you been sitting on?
What vision has been stirring inside you that you've been too afraid to act on?
What project have you been postponing because you don't feel *ready* or *qualified*?

Stop waiting for the perfect moment. There is no perfect moment.
Stop waiting for permission. You don't need it.
Stop doubting your ability. You'll grow into it.
Your ideas are gifts. But they only matter if you move on them.

Faith Moves First

The path won't always be clear. Sometimes, you won't see the destination until you start walking. But being a forerunner means having the courage to move anyway.

It means trusting that God can take your small idea and turn it into something beyond your wildest imagination.

So, the question isn't whether you have what it takes. The real question is: Are you willing to go first?

Because when you do, you might just find that the road you've been waiting for was waiting for you to build it.

That said, when you go first, not everything will go as planned. But remember—what looks like failure may be the foundation for your next move.

Presumptuous in Practice

💡 **Reflect:** Identify an idea you've shelved out of fear.

✍️ **Journal Prompt:** What would it look like to act on it without permission?

▶▶ **Bold Move:** Draft a basic plan—just the first 3 steps.

💡 **Reframe:** If I go first, who might find their way because I moved?

dib

13

It's Not What It Looks Like

¶¶

Juli-Anne and I got engaged on December 10, 2008. She was working at a global investment firm, and I was juggling two jobs—an insurance company during the day and Home Depot in the evenings. We were saving for our wedding, our honeymoon, and the new place we planned to move into. Life was full, busy, and demanding. But even as I chose to grind through long days, something inside me was restless.

I had always been drawn to teaching—to the idea of inspiring young people and helping them navigate their most formative years. I thought maybe I'd go to teacher's college—carve out a career in the classroom, make my impact that way.

But God had different plans.

When the Calling Calls

During our premarital counseling with our officiating pastor, he asked me a question that caught me completely off guard: "Have you ever considered becoming a youth pastor?"

The question came out of nowhere. I hadn't been to Bible college, hadn't trained for ministry, and I certainly didn't see myself behind a pulpit. Yet, he saw something in me that I hadn't yet considered. He sensed that the way I was wired—the energy I carried, the creative edge, the way I connected with young people through things like *The J.A.M!* and S4—might not thrive inside the constraints of a traditional classroom. He saw a calling that needed more room to move. He told me the church where he once served was looking for a youth pastor.

His question didn't offend me—but it unsettled me. It resonated with something deep down in me. Because even though the thought of pastoring didn't excite me, it also wouldn't leave me alone. It just lingered there in my mind, nudging me toward something I didn't yet understand.

When Juli-Anne and I got back from our honeymoon, we decided to visit the church where the opportunity had opened up. I didn't walk in with any grand expectations. I wasn't looking for a sign. But there, sitting in the pews, something stirred—not a fiery passion, not an overwhelming clarity, but a quiet conviction.

This is where I need to be.

I didn't fully understand it, but I knew I needed to take the next step.

Qualified by Calling

By early 2010, I had multiple meetings with the church leadership. They were intrigued by my unconventional journey and felt I could bring something fresh to their youth ministry. After a few discussions, they offered me the position—with one condition: I had to earn a degree in theology. They would cover the expenses.

Once again, I wasn't qualified for the role—not by conventional standards. But deep down, I knew that God doesn't call the qualified; He qualifies the called. I was clear. This was my next step, even though it didn't make sense on paper.

Presumptuous means moving forward before all the details are figured out.

So, I took the leap. And just like that, a new chapter began.

Pulpit, Pampers, Progress

From the very beginning, God spoke clearly:

> *"Don't try to be what you think a pastor should be. I've called you to be you."*

Teenagers have a built-in radar for inauthenticity anyway—they know when you're faking it. So, I decided I'd be 100% myself—and that choice made all the difference.

Over the next six and a half years, I poured myself into the work:

- Learning how to counsel young people through difficult seasons
- Planning community events that connected faith and culture
- Preaching sermons that were raw, real, and relevant
- Mentoring youth leaders in ways that built trust, depth, and lasting connection

I grew as a person, as a leader, as a husband and, I became a father.

All three of our daughters were born during this time. Fatherhood deepened everything—my faith, my sense of purpose, and my love for my wife.

Many of the young people I mentored during those years remain in our lives today—some have even asked Juli-Anne and me to officiate their weddings. The impact of that season was profound.

But something was shifting.

Exit Signs

One morning in January 2016, I stepped out of the shower, glanced in the mirror, and felt something heavy drop into my spirit:

My time here is done.

It was so clear I told Juli-Anne right away. I had no reason to believe it—nothing had happened—but I just knew what I sensed.

At a staff retreat the following month, on a break, I called Juli-Anne and said "We won't be here at Christmas."

The months that followed were filled with tension and unrest within the church. In April, a contentious Annual General Meeting. Leadership struggles. A growing sense that things were misaligned.

Then, one night in June, I woke up at 4:22 a.m. God prompted me to write a letter. I got out of bed, sat down, and wrote four pages—a letter to the leadership that felt like it was being dictated to me.

The message? The church had lost sight of its purpose. It needed to refocus on serving the community instead of itself.

When I finished writing, I sat with it for a moment—staring at the words that had poured out like a download. I felt a strange mix of certainty and tension. I knew the letter wasn't just my opinion; it was Spirit-led. But I also knew the weight of what I was about to do. This wasn't just feedback—it was an indictment.

At first, the response was positive. Some members of the leadership said I had voiced concerns they too shared—but hadn't dared to say out loud. For a moment, I thought, *Maybe this is the shift we need.*

But then, the atmosphere changed. The letter, which had been seen at first as a call for realignment, was suddenly twisted into something else. Criticism came in waves. Tension increased.

Had someone reframed my words? Had seeds of doubt been planted?

Shortly after, I was called into a meeting with several members of the leadership team—seven in total. I thought we were gathering to clarify, to align. But from the moment I sat down, it became clear: this wasn't a conversation. It was a condemnation.

They questioned my character, my motives, even my calling. I was called arrogant. Ineffective. I was told that, for the past six years, my leadership had done more harm than good. At one point, a church elder—someone I had served alongside for years—told me to shut up.

I sat there, stunned, absorbing blow after blow. Not one person spoke in my defense.

That night, driving home, I called Juli-Anne. I could barely get the words out. The tears came hard and fast. The pain—of being misunderstood, dishonored, and discarded—was suffocating. She had to ask me to pull the car over.

That night was the clearest confirmation I'd ever received: this is what it means to be called presumptuous. To be labeled dangerous because you dared to challenge the status quo. To be misunderstood not because you were careless, but because you were convicted. And this—this is why we have to reclaim the word.

Whether it was misunderstanding, manipulation, or just the discomfort of hard truth, one thing became undeniable.

The whisper I heard in January—the one I couldn't explain, the one I almost doubted—was now thundering.

My time here is done.

Exit Wounds, Entry Points

In October, I made the decision to resign. The very next day, God gave us the download for our next step.

We don't always want to move without a full itinerary. But a presumptuous life doesn't wait for all the dots to connect. It steps. It trusts. It adjusts mid-air.

God was teaching us something deeper than obedience. He was teaching us *agility*—the ability to pivot with purpose, to respond without resistance, to trust without total clarity.

From the outside, leaving the church looked like failure. Like rejection. Like everything I had worked to build was unraveling.

But in truth? It was alignment. It was release. It was divine choreography that required me to move, even if it didn't make sense. Because sometimes, the shift doesn't *look* spiritual. It looks like grief. It feels like loss.

But that doesn't mean it isn't God.

We assume that longevity equals success, that staying means faithfulness. But God sometimes assigns seasons not for permanence—but for preparation. For stretching. For sharpening. For shaping.

You gather tools. You gain wisdom. You outgrow spaces that once fit just fine. Then, when it's time, the exit becomes an entry—to something bolder, broader, and built by obedience.

Maybe you feel it now. A nudge. A whisper. A restlessness that won't go away.

And maybe the reason you haven't moved is because you're waiting for full clarity.

But presumptuous doesn't wait for guarantees. It moves with God—even when the map is missing. Presumptuous means being agile enough to leave when staying would feel safer. It means shifting *with* the Spirit, even when others don't understand. It means obedience that offends human logic.

Leaving isn't always escape. Sometimes, it's evolution.

And on the other side of obedience?
There's room to build something bold.

Are you willing to trust the shift? Even when life shifts, the call is simple: stay presumptuous.

Presumptuous in Practice

Q **Reflect:** Think of a moment that looked like failure but became foundation.

✍ **Journal Prompt:** Write down 3 lessons it taught you.

▶ **Bold Move:** Share that story with someone who needs hope.

💡 **Reframe:** Ask: Is this moment the end—or a doorway in disguise?

dllb

14
—

Stay
Presumptuous

'm writing this book in a season of my life that is still very much presumptuous. Every day, I'm listening to my gut, responding to the needs around me, and stepping into opportunities that weren't on my radar but align with a bigger vision.

Before we move forward, let's go back—because some journeys begin long before we realize we're on them.

In 2013, life for Juli-Anne and me was settled. We had two daughters, Akeylah and Amaya, and were living in a two-bedroom townhouse condo in Mississauga. Moving wasn't something we were actively considering. But one rainy day, on a whim, we decided to look at model homes. It wasn't a serious pursuit, just curiosity. Yet, before we set out, we prayed a simple prayer: "Lord, *light the way*."

We drove from sales office to sales office, heading further north with each stop. Nothing felt right. Then, we remembered a friend had mentioned a town called Shelburne, about an hour north of Mississauga. We had never considered it before, but something about the name lingered in our minds. So, we pulled up the GPS and set out in that direction.

As we drove up Highway 10, with an overcast sky and rain still drizzling, we looked off into the distance. Right at the top of the highway, where the road curves westward toward Shelburne, the sun broke through the clouds. *Crepuscular rays*—those streaks of sunlight that burst through gaps in the clouds—lit up the town like a spotlight from heaven. It wasn't just a subtle change in the weather; it felt like divine confirmation. We looked at each other to make sure we were both seeing the same thing. It was almost cinematic, like a joke, but somehow completely real. A moment of clarity.

That's the thing about being presumptuous—you don't always have the full picture, but you recognize when the moment calls for you to move. We weren't just presumptuous in considering this move for our family; we were bold enough to invite seven of our closest friends to move up as well. It was a big ask, but we were more excited to share the opportunity than we were afraid of their "no." Worst-case scenario, they could move for a year, hate it, and sell at a profit to move back to the city. But to our surprise—and perhaps theirs—they agreed. One by one, they took that leap with us, trusting that this move was part of something bigger.

We purchased our home in 2013 and had to wait two years for it to be built. By 2015, we moved in, and a few months later, our third daughter, Alexandra, was born. We were still commuting back to Mississauga for church, but we couldn't help but notice a need right where we lived. That *download* I mentioned? Well, in the fall of 2016, God gave us the vision to create a space for youth, and use the arts as our tool to connect, inspire, and empower them. On October 6, 2016, we registered the charity, Streams Community Hub.

Around that same time, my brother-in-law, Kervin, had some apparel printing equipment and asked if I could help with some graphic design work. I said yes, not thinking much of it. But very quickly, Juli-Anne and I saw an opportunity to optimize the business model. Kervin had originally planned to start his own clothing line, but we saw that the real opportunity was in creating custom apparel for others—businesses, schools, and organizations that needed branded merchandise. He agreed, and before we knew it, he moved all his equipment into our basement in Shelburne, and we got to work.

From the very first shirt I pressed, I thought: *This could be a really cool job for young people, giving them their first work experience.* And at the same time, I saw the potential for this to grow into something that could financially support Streams. What if we could build our own sustainability—through business, not begging?

That's exactly what happened.

By 2018, we rebranded the business as Town Tees, focusing on two things:

1. Hiring and training young people, giving them valuable first-job experience, and,
2. Letting our customers know that their purchases helped support Streams.

The social enterprise model became the heartbeat of our business, and as Town Tees grew, its ability to financially support Streams grew too.

Today, we're still walking this leg of the journey out. Over the last eight years, Streams has gone from running seasonal camps in borrowed spaces to offering year-round programming in our own 3,600-square-foot facility. It's become a staple in the community, a favourite among parents and youth. We're receiving grants and funding that are positioning us to become a lasting pillar in the region. And

Town Tees has played a significant role in that.

And now, Town Tees is expanding again. In 2025, we opened our second location in Alliston, Ontario. Expansion wasn't on my radar—but at some point, I had envisioned a franchise model for Town Tees—a way to bring this social enterprise to more communities, creating more youth employment opportunities and greater sustainability for Streams. But sometimes, the future arrives sooner than expected. When the opportunity to open a second location presented itself, we recognized that the space was ideal and the timing was right. I didn't say yes because it was easy—I said yes because I had a strong team behind me.

This moment is just another example of why you have to stay presumptuous. You don't wait until you have all the details. You don't wait for certainty. You don't wait for comfort. You listen, you move, and you trust that clarity will come in motion.

I don't know what the future holds for Town Tees, or Streams. But I *do* know that we will continue redefining what service, education, and youth engagement through the arts can do to transform a community. I know that every leap we've taken has led to something greater than we originally envisioned. And I know that by continuing to live presumptuously—by

trusting the vision, moving boldly, and embracing uncertainty—we will create something that outlives us.

*Presumptuous choices require risk—and risk always invites
fear. But fear doesn't get the final say.*

Presumptuous in Practice

○ **Reflect:** What area of life are you overthinking, where you need to move?

✍ **Journal Prompt:** Set a deadline for a decision you've been avoiding.

▶ **Bold Move:** Create a presumptuous calendar: 1 bold step per week.

💡 **Reframe:** Am I stuck or just stalling because I'm scared?

dlb

15

Don't Give Fear The Final Say

¶¶

Fear is a masterful storyteller. It crafts elaborate, detailed narratives in our minds, painting vivid pictures of all the ways things could go wrong. It tells us we'll fail, that people will judge us, that we'll lose everything if we take the risk. It plays on our insecurities and whispers that we aren't ready, aren't good enough, aren't qualified. And if we listen long enough, fear wins.

I've had to battle fear in nearly every presumptuous decision I've made. It has tried to stop me from stepping out, from making bold moves, from pursuing the things I knew deep down I was meant to do. And sometimes, if I'm honest, it has succeeded—at least temporarily. But I've also learned something about fear: It doesn't tell the truth.

Fear is a liar, and it's also a gatekeeper. Every time I've pushed past fear, there was something worthwhile on the other side.

Every single time. That's why I now see fear as an indicator that I'm on the edge of something important. If fear shows up, it usually means I'm stepping into new territory—into something bigger than what I've known before.

Fear Almost Stopped Me

There have been times when fear nearly made the call instead of me. Town Tees might look like a bold move now, but there was a moment—early on—when fear almost made me play it safe instead of betting on what I believed.

When Town Tees first started, it was in the basement. It was gritty and unpolished, but it worked. Orders were coming in, and business was good. But I knew that kind of setup wasn't built to scale. Customers coming through the front door of our house didn't feel right. Hiring help and having them pass by our living room to get to "work" felt even less right. We were operating like a real business—but from inside a very personal space. Something had to change.

The opportunity came when Streams signed the lease on our new facility. There was space in the building, and it made perfect sense for Town Tees to move in. We could finally look and operate like a business, and the rent we paid could help cover some of Streams' lease commitment. It was the logical next step. And for a while, it worked.

Don't Give Fear The Final Say

But then we grew. Fast.

Within a year, we were bursting at the seams, and Town Tees started to creep into corners of Streams where it shouldn't have been. We needed our own space. Again.

Our landlords—great people—offered us another unit in the plaza. We sat down with them over dinner to talk terms. And I'll be honest, I was shook. The growth had been fast. The responsibility had gotten heavy.

I started to doubt myself.

I could feel the questions rising:
Am I in over my head?
Are we doing too much?
What if we can't sustain this?

I was about to open my mouth and let fear start speaking on my behalf. But before I could say a word, Juli-Anne reached under the table and placed her hand gently on my knee. No words. Just presence. Calm. Clarity.

A few minutes later, while the landlords were distracted chatting with the waiter, she leaned in and whispered,

"Not here. Not now. We're good. We will figure this out."
And just like that, faith held its ground. Fear didn't get to speak that night. We made the deal. We moved. And we haven't looked back since.

Fear Has a Cost—So Does Playing Small

That moment made something crystal clear for me: fear doesn't just keep you from doing something bold—it lures you into something small.

We often think of bold decisions as risky. But we rarely talk about the risk of playing it safe. Staying small has a cost too—and it might be the most expensive one of all.

Every time you downplay your abilities...
Every time you sit on an idea because it's not fully formed yet...
Every time you shrink to make others comfortable...

You're paying for it. With your potential. With your peace. With your purpose.

We think we're being cautious. Wise. Responsible. But what we're actually doing is hiding.

What Playing Small Really Costs

1. **It costs you your potential.** There are gifts inside you—visions, ideas, businesses, songs, solutions—that may never see the light of day if you let fear run the show. Playing small may feel safe, but it's robbing you of who you could become.

2. **It costs others, too.** The people who were meant to benefit from your boldness—the young people Streams was built for, the first-time employees at Town Tees, the lives that were supposed to be touched—they miss out when you don't step up.

3. **It costs you your peace.** You might avoid the stress of risk, but you'll live with the *slow ache of regret*. You'll always wonder what might've happened if you had just moved.

Fear Doesn't Leave—But You Get Stronger

Here's the truth: Fear doesn't magically disappear just because you've chosen to be bold once. It's not a one-time battle; it's an ongoing war. Every new level of life brings new fears. The first time I launched a business, I was scared. The first time I stood on stage to preach, I was scared. The first time I spoke to a room full of young people who needed real answers, I was scared. Even writing this book—I had to push past fear to put my thoughts onto these pages, and into the world.

But here's the good news: The more you face fear, the weaker its grip becomes. You grow stronger. You learn that fear is predictable. You learn its patterns and its tactics. And eventually, you learn that you don't have to obey it.

The One You Feed Wins

Fear and faith are two sides of the same coin. Both require you to believe in something you can't see yet. *Fear asks you to believe in worst-case scenarios. Faith asks you to believe in best-case scenarios.* One will keep you stuck; the other will move you forward.

So, the question is: Which one are you feeding?

Here's a practical exercise: The next time fear feeds worst-case scenarios, counter it with a list of best-case scenarios. Write down everything that could go right if you take that step. What if you actually succeed? What if the opportunity leads to something greater than you imagined? What if people rally around you and support you? What if this decision sets your future on an entirely new, better trajectory?

It's not about ignoring risks or being reckless—it's about choosing to focus on the possibility instead of the problem.

Do It Anyway

Presumptuous doesn't mean fearless—it means moving forward despite fear. It means making a decision to act, even when your hands are shaking and your heart is racing.

Think about the things you've been hesitating about. The decisions you know you need to make but have been putting off because fear keeps telling you to wait.

Ask yourself:
- Is fear actually protecting me, or is it just keeping me comfortable?
- Am I letting fear stop me from stepping into something I'm called to do?
- If I wasn't afraid, what would I do right now?

Then, do it. Even if you're scared. Even if it's uncomfortable. Act. Move. Speak. Start. Whatever it is—take the first step.

Because the truth is, fear will always have a voice. But it doesn't have to have the final say.

Not anymore.

Now let's look at how boldness shifts your circle.

Presumptuous in Practice

○ **Reflect:** Write down your current top 3 fears.

✎ **Journal Prompt:** List 1 best-case scenario for each.

▶ **Bold Move:** Take one courageous action—small, but meaningful—today.

💡 **Reframe:** Ask: What would faith say if fear weren't talking over it?

dlb

16

Presumptuous in Relationships

¶|¶

Relationships are the foundation of life. No matter how bold, gifted, or visionary you are—this journey isn't travelled alone. And when you choose to live a presumptuous life—when you take risks, step into the unknown, and dare to believe in things others can't yet see—it inevitably affects the people around you.

Some will champion you. Some will question you. Some will drift away. The moment you step out of the mold, your relationships will be tested.

When People Don't See the Vision

One of the hardest things about taking bold steps is realizing that not everyone will see what you see. There have been times in my life when I was so sure—so completely convinced—of a vision, and yet, the people closest to me were hesitant. They weren't trying to discourage me.

They just couldn't see what I saw.

I've learned that this is natural.

Not everyone is meant to understand your calling, because it wasn't given to them. It was given to you.

When Juli-Anne and I first felt the call to start Streams, it didn't make sense to a lot of people. We were leaving a comfortable, stable life for something uncertain. People asked us practical questions:

"How will you fund it?"
"What if it doesn't work?"
"Why not just serve in an existing organization instead of building something new?"

They weren't wrong for asking. These were valid concerns. But if we had waited for everyone to fully understand or approve of our decision, we would have never taken the first step. That's the thing about living presumptuously— sometimes you have to move before the validation comes.

Losing Relationships Along the Way

Some relationships won't survive the journey. I've lost friend- ships because of the bold choices I've made. Not out of conflict or malice, but because growth often changes the dynamics of relationships. When you step out in faith, it does two things: It inspires some and intimidates others.

Some people will be drawn to your boldness, encouraged to pursue their own dreams. Others will feel confronted by it, like a mirror reflecting their own hesitations and fears. Sometimes, when people aren't ready to move themselves, they distance from those who do.

I've learned that this is okay.

Not everyone is meant to go with you to the next level. Some friendships are for a season, and when that season shifts, the relationship does too. It doesn't mean the friendship wasn't real. Or that there's bad blood. It just means your paths have diverged.

And if you spend all your time trying to hold onto relationships that are no longer aligned with where you're going, you'll slow yourself down.

The Power of the Right People

While some relationships fade, others deepen.

The beauty of living a presumptuous life is that when you step into your purpose, the right people will find you.

Over the years, I've met people who *get it*—people who have the same fire, the same vision, the same willingness to take risks. These are the relationships that sharpen you, that challenge you, that remind you why you started.

And then there's *marriage.*

I can't talk about relationships and bold decision-making without talking about Juli-Anne.

From the beginning, we've had to figure out what it means to be two strong, visionary people doing life together. There have been moments when I've had to convince her of something I knew we needed to do, and moments when she's been the one pushing me forward.

One of the biggest lessons we've learned is this: Bold decision-making in marriage requires trust. It requires trusting that even when one of us doesn't fully see the vision, we can still trust the person who does.

There have been times when I had to move forward with something that made Juli-Anne nervous—times when she had to rely not on her own understanding, but on the confidence, she had in God and in me. And the same is true in reverse.

But that trust is built over time. It comes from proving—again and again—that we are on the same team, that we are moving toward the same goal, that even if one of us can't see *how* something will work, we trust *why* we're doing it.

When People Think You're Crazy

If you live presumptuously long enough, you'll hear some version of this:

"You're crazy."

"You're doing too much."

"You should slow down."

"You should play it safe."

But what's crazier? Taking bold steps toward your purpose, or living a life you know is smaller than what you were made for?

At the end of the day, the people who misunderstand you, the ones who doubt you, the ones who tell you to *just be realistic*—they don't have to live with your regrets. You do.

So if it comes down to pleasing people or pursuing purpose, **choose purpose**.

If it comes down to keeping a relationship that holds you back or stepping into what God has for you, **choose what God has for you**.

If it comes down to being liked or being obedient to what you know is right, **choose obedience**.

What Relationships Need in a Bold Life

If you want to live boldly *and* maintain healthy relationships, here's what I've learned you need:

1. **Clear Communication** – Don't assume people understand your vision. Explain it. Share your heart. Let them in.
2. **Grace** – Not everyone will see what you see, and that's okay. Give them time—and if they still don't get it, release them with grace.
3. **A Core Support System** – Surround yourself with at least a few people who believe in you, who encourage you, and who remind you why you started.
4. **Wisdom** – Not everyone is meant to speak into your vision. Be selective about who you take advice from.
5. **Trust in Your Calling** – At the end of the day, your vision is yours. No one else is responsible for believing in it. You are.

The People Who Stay

Some relationships will change.

Some people will walk away.

Some friendships will fade.

But the people who stay? They're the ones who are meant to. They are the ones who will celebrate your wins, challenge you when you need it, and walk with you through every bold step. And when you find those people? Hold onto them. Invest in those relationships. Because in this presumptuous life, you'll need them as much as they need you.

Food for Thought

Presumptuous living will test your relationships. But it will also reveal who's truly meant to walk this journey with you. Some relationships can't go where you're going—and that's okay. What matters is that you walk honestly, love courageously, and give your future circle someone worth following.

Relationships may shape us, but what sustains us are the deeper anchors—seven pillars that hold everything up. Let's name them.

Presumptuous in Practice

○ **Reflect:** Audit your relationships: who energizes vs. who drains?

✍ **Journal Prompt:** Identify one brave conversation you've been avoiding.

▶ **Bold Move:** Have it—with grace, love, and clarity.

💡 **Reframe:** Ask: Do my connections support my calling?

dlb

17

The Seven Pillars of Presumptuousness

qIp

As I reflected on the stories and lessons in this book, I realized there are certain key components essential to living a presumptuous life. They're not the only tools you'll need—but they're a strong foundation. Living a life that stretches beyond comfort, that embraces the extraordinary, requires more than bold ideas and leaps of faith.

It demands seven essential pillars:

- Integrity
- Joy
- Discipline
- Agility
- Conviction
- Faith
- Action

Each one plays a crucial role in turning dreams into reality and navigating life's uncertainties with confidence and purpose. As you consider them, ask yourself:

How am I intentionally nurturing these areas in my own life?

Integrity

Integrity is the cornerstone of a presumptuous life.

It's about being true to your values and principles, even when no one is watching. It means aligning your actions with your beliefs—making sure your public persona matches your private character.

Living with integrity means making choices based on what's right, not what's easy. It's about building trust—not just with others, but with yourself. Because when you know you're standing on a solid foundation, you gain the confidence to move boldly in life.

For me, integrity has been non-negotiable. Whether in business, ministry, or personal relationships, it has been the principle that has kept me grounded. Integrity isn't just about avoiding the wrong; it's about actively choosing the right, even when it costs you something.

Discipline

Discipline is what turns potential into progress.

It's easy to be excited about a dream at the start—but the real challenge is showing up every single day when no one is watching. Discipline keeps you moving forward, even when motivation wanes.

Discipline is:
- Consistency—Doing the work, even when you don't feel like it.
- Focus—Avoiding distractions that derail progress.
- Perseverance—Pushing through obstacles without quitting.

Streams. Town Tees. S4. Marriage. Fatherhood. This book. Every major achievement in my life is built on discipline. It's not glamorous, but it's what separates those who dream from those who achieve.

Conviction

Conviction is the fuel behind bold decisions.

It's the unshakable belief that what you're pursuing is worth it—even when the path is unclear.

Have you ever watched someone doing something, but it lacked believability? That's because it lacked conviction.

On the other hand, have you ever been moved to tears by a song or a movie? That's the power of conviction—it resonates and compels.

Looking back, every major leap I've taken—whether it was starting *The J.A.M!*, launching Streams, or moving to Shelburne—was driven by conviction. I didn't always have certainty, but I had belief.

If you lack conviction, you'll hesitate. And hesitation *kills* dreams.

Action

Action is what separates dreamers from doers.

It's not enough to want something or talk about it. You have to move—even if you don't have all the answers.

Living presumptuously means acting on faith, not waiting for clarity. I've learned that waiting for the perfect moment often leads to missed opportunities. Some of my biggest leaps happened before I had everything figured out. But by taking that first step, the next steps became clearer. Action brings momentum. *Clarity comes in motion.*

⚏ Joy ⚏

Joy is what sustains you on the journey.

Pursuing big dreams comes with challenges, setbacks, and hard work. But if you lose your sense of joy, the weight of the journey can crush you.

Joy is sacred resistance in a world obsessed with hustle, hierarchy, and hyper-performance. It's not reactive. It's rooted. Joy doesn't mean ignoring pain—it means choosing gladness in the presence of it. It's not something you feel when life is good; it's something you produce when your life is grounded in God.

It was joy that carried me through the pushback after writing that letter to the church leadership.
It was joy that made stage lights feel like home.
It was joy that let me keep building, even when logic said to quit.

Joy allows you to:
- Stay motivated when things get tough.
- Find pleasure in the process, not just the outcome.
- Maintain a light heart even in the face of struggle.

Joy is a fruit of the Spirit—and in a life as presumptuous as this one, you'll need to keep choosing it, daily.

≋ Agility ≋

Agility is the ability to pivot when necessary.

Being rigid in your thinking can cause you to miss opportunities. Life is rarely a straight path—you must be willing to adjust.

Sometimes, what we think is the right way isn't the best way. Juli-Anne reminds me of this all the time—she's great at seeing when we need to shift directions. Her agility has saved us from getting stuck in outdated plans.

Being agile means knowing when to:
- Let go of a plan that isn't working.
- Shift your strategy when new opportunities arise.
- Stay open to unexpected paths that may be even better than your original vision.

The pursuit of greatness is rarely linear. The ability to bend without breaking is what keeps you moving forward.

≋ Faith ≋

Faith is what holds everything together.

It's trusting in something greater—in God's plan—even when the way forward isn't clear.

Faith:

- Anchors you in times of uncertainty.
- Gives you strength to keep going when obstacles arise.
- Allows you to dream bigger, knowing you are supported.

For me, faith has been everything. It has fueled every major decision I've made, given me courage to take bold steps and provided peace when things felt uncertain.

Without faith, doubt will keep you stuck. But with faith, you move forward—even when you can't see the whole path.

Start With One

Presumptuous doesn't mean reckless. It means bold, courageous, and unafraid to reach for the extraordinary. These seven pillars—Integrity, Discipline, Conviction, Action, Joy, Agility, and Faith—have been the foundation of my journey.

Now, the question is: Which of these pillars do you need to strengthen in your own life?

Start with one. Strengthen it. Let it shift how you carry the weight of your own presumptuous life.

The pillars are personal, but their impact is generational. Let's explore that next.

Presumptuous in Practice

💡   **Reflect:** Score yourself 1–10 on each of the seven pillars.

✍🏼   **Journal Prompt:** Pick your lowest pillar—commit to nurturing it this month.

▶▶   **Bold Move:** Create a micro-habit that supports growth in that area.

💡   **Reframe:** Which pillar is holding up the least weight right now?

dlb

18

The Presumptuous Life Beyond You

¶¶

L iving a presumptuous life isn't just about what you accomplish in your lifetime. It's about what you leave behind.

At some point, every one of us has to ask: *What will remain when I'm gone?*

Not just in terms of success or recognition, but in impact. In the lives touched. In the ideas planted. In the foundation laid for those who come after us.

A truly presumptuous life doesn't stop with you. It extends beyond your years. It becomes something that outlives your presence, shaping the world in ways you may never fully see.

Leaving an Inheritance

I think about my daughters a lot when it comes to legacy.

I don't just want them to have a good life. I want them to know that they have the power to shape their own lives. I want them to live boldly, to trust their instincts, to step out in faith even when it doesn't make sense. I want them to embrace a level of presumptuousness that allows them to walk into rooms with confidence, to take up space without apology, to pursue their passions with full conviction.

I don't care what careers they choose, whether they follow in my footsteps or chart their own course entirely. What I *do* care about is that they never shrink themselves. That they never settle for less than what they were created to carry. That they never let fear be the thing that keeps them from moving forward.

If they grow up believing that faith and action can move mountains, that their lives have purpose, that God has placed within them everything they need to fulfill their destiny— then I will know I've done my job.

Because my legacy isn't just what I *leave* for them. It's what I *build* in them.

Bigger Than Business

When Juli-Anne and I started Streams Community Hub, it wasn't just about creating programs for kids. It was about shifting the culture—from the ground up.

We wanted to build something that could sustain itself long after we're gone. Something that wouldn't just exist for a few years and fade away, but would grow, expand, and evolve with each new generation.

I want Streams to be a place that continues to unlock creativity in young people, a space where kids feel safe, seen, and inspired. I want it to be a launching pad for future leaders, artists, entrepreneurs, and innovators. I want it to be a legacy of opportunity—where kids who might have otherwise been overlooked are given the chance to discover their full potential.

Town Tees, too, is bigger than a business.

I don't just want it to be a company that prints shirts. I want it to be a training ground for young people who need their first job, who need to learn what it means to take ownership, to develop work ethic, to see themselves as capable and creative.

My hope is that years from now, young people who got their start at Town Tees will be running their own businesses, launching their own ventures, and carrying forward the mindset that work isn't just about making money—it's about making impact.

And ultimately, I want both Streams and Town Tees to remind to every kid who walks through our doors: You don't need to wait for a seat. You can build the table.

The Responsibility of Legacy

Legacy isn't something that just happens. It's something you build. And building it requires intentionality. It requires thinking beyond the present, beyond your own lifetime. It requires making decisions not just for your benefit, but for the benefit of those who will come after you.

That means leading with integrity. Making choices that align with your values. Investing in people, not just projects. Pouring into the next generation, even when no one's watching. Even when the return isn't guaranteed.

It means living in such a way that your life becomes a blueprint for others to follow. It means refusing to play small.

Because your legacy is not just in what you achieve. It's in *who you become.*

At the end of the day, none of us live forever.

The Presumptuous Life Beyond You

One day, people will sit around telling stories about you. What will they say?

Will they say you played it safe? Stayed inside the lines? Avoided the edge? That you never took risks, never stretched beyond what was comfortable?

Or will they say you *believed*—that you took audacious steps, that you lived boldly, that you left the world better than you found it?

Will they say you *poured* into others, that you built something meaningful, that you left an imprint that couldn't be erased?

I want my legacy to be one of *faith in action.*

I want my children, my family, my community to know that I lived with intention. That I didn't let fear make my decisions. That I refused to settle for a life of mediocrity.

And I want *you* to consider the same.
Because the presumptuous life is never just about you. It's about what lives after you.

A presumptuous life—one lived with faith, boldness, and conviction—naturally spills over into legacy. When you live fully, when you push past fear, when you act on your purpose, you create ripples that extend beyond your years.

So don't just live for the now. Live for the generations that will come after you. Live in such a way that when people speak of you, they will say, *because of them, I believed I could too.* Live in such a way that your boldness becomes someone else's permission slip.

That is a legacy worth building. That is a life worth living.

By now, you've walked through the stories, the lessons, the challenges, and the triumphs that make up the presumptuous life. You've seen what happens when boldness collides with faith, when action overtakes hesitation, when conviction pushes past the barriers of fear and doubt.

But this book isn't really about me. It's about *you.*

Everything you've read so far is meaningless if it doesn't translate into action.

So let me ask you directly: What are you going to do *today* to start living presumptuously?

Not next week. Not when you "feel ready." Not when you have all the answers.

Today.

Because nothing changes until *you* change.

You've walked through the pages—now walk it out. Reflection is powerful. But action builds legacy. Let's turn reflection into a roadmap.

Presumptuous in Practice

💡 **Reflect:** Write your legacy in 5 sentences.

✍️ **Journal Prompt:** What seeds can you plant now that will outlive you?

▶ **Bold Move:** Mentor or uplift someone younger this week.

💡 **Reframe:** Ask: What will echo when my voice is gone?

dlb

Your
Presumptuous
Life Map

ongratulations.You've made it through the book. The stories, insights, and challenges you've walked through weren't just reflections — they were *activation points*. You've been equipped with tools to live boldly, to make uncommon moves, and to become someone who doesn't wait for permission.

Now it's time to **put it all in motion**. This is the moment the book stops being something you read—and becomes the life you live.

Are you ready?

1 Your New Operating System: 'Presumptuous Beliefs
Living presumptuously means you **stop waiting**—for clarity, for timing, for permission. It means you move in **constant faith**, grounded in *unchangeable truth*.

Here are a few presumptuous beliefs to adopt as your **new compass**:

- I don't need permission to move in purpose.
- I build what I don't yet see.
- Fear doesn't get the final say.
- My gifts are valid, needed, and worthy of visibility.
- Obedience matters more than certainty.
- Discomfort is a sign that I'm growing.
- I'm not behind—I'm right on time for my assignment.
- God isn't waiting for me to be perfect—just willing.

Now add your own. Name the truths you'll live by. Let these become the soundtrack of your boldest life.

2 **Design Your Presumptuous Life Map.** What are the key areas in your life right now that require **more boldness, more faith, and more action**? Choose three. (You can add more later.)

For each one, define:

- The boldest vision you have for this area
- One small but bold action you'll take this week
- One limiting belief you're committed to challenge

Examples:

Calling
- *Vision:* I will redefine my career to reflect my passion for helping others.
- *Bold Action:* Apply for the dream job.
- *Limiting Belief:* I'm not qualified.

Relationships
- *Vision:* I will build deep, authentic connections with people who align with my values.
- *Bold Action:* Have a vulnerable, honest conversation with a friend.
- *Limiting Belief:* I don't deserve that kind of connection.

Health
- *Vision:* I will live with vitality, balance, and care for my body like it matters.
- *Bold Action:* Start a 20-minute walk + meal prep plan.
- *Limiting Belief:* I don't have the time.

Start there. Then expand. **This is your map.**

3 Make It Real. Dreams die in delay. **Boldness needs evidence.** Choose at least one of these actions to bring your map to life:

- **Craft a Manifesto:** Write your personal mission statement — a declaration of who you are, what you believe, and the legacy you're building.
- **Message Your Future Self:** Record a video or write a letter to your future self (6 months from now), affirming your commitment to the journey.
- **Share Your Story:** Choose one chapter of your life and share it with someone you trust. Let your vulnerability build accountability.

Final Charge

You've made it to the end. But really?

This is the beginning.

You've identified who you are.

You've claimed your values.

You've mapped your way forward.

Now—go live it.

Don't wait for the perfect moment.
Don't wait for full clarity.

Move as if heaven and earth are already aligned with your bold vision.

Act as if the impossible is just your next logical step.

Your Presumptuous Life Map

You don't need another confirmation.

You *are* the confirmation.

So walk it out.

Make noise.

Take up space.

Build what doesn't yet exist.

Show up presumptuously—because the world is waiting on your courage.

Epilogue:
Always Ask
the Wife

¶⫿P

If you really want to know what a man is like—beyond the words he speaks, the image he presents, or the persona he carefully crafts—**ask his wife**.

Watch her face when he talks. Observe how she moves through spaces where he stands. Listen for the unspoken testimony in her posture, in the ease (or effort) with which she exists beside him. It's easy to fool an audience—to impress those who only see fragments of a life. But the people closest to you, the ones who witness the private moments? They carry the truth. And they don't always speak it with words.

So here's mine.

Everything Andrew has written in this book—his audacity to dream, his refusal to settle, his relentless faith in what *could be*—he lives it. The values he espouses here, the presumptuous life he invites others into, aren't just philosophies. They are the daily rhythms of his existence. I've seen him bet on the impossible when logic said quit. I have watched him step into rooms with nothing but conviction and come out with doors flung open. I've stood beside him—sometimes shaking my head at the sheer boldness of it all, but never doubting he meant every word.

But here's the thing: Andrew doesn't just live these values for himself.

His highest calling is to see *others* rise.

He's not only presumptuous in pursuit of his own destiny—he's relentless, often at great personal sacrifice, in creating avenues, atmospheres, and platforms for others to step into theirs. He believes, deeply, that greatness is meant to be drawn out. That potential should never stay dormant. That no one should remain bound by the limitations imposed on them—by society, circumstance, or self-doubt.

This is especially true for young people. But really, it applies to anyone in his sphere. If you're within his reach, he will challenge you, push you, call you higher—not for his sake, but for yours.

And while it may be frustrating at times to live with someone so *utterly unwilling* to let you settle... It is also the most profound gift.

Because to be loved like that—to have someone insist you step into *all* you were meant to be—is rare. And it is powerful.

So if you're reading this and wondering whether the principles in these pages actually hold weight in real life, I can answer without hesitation:

Yes.

And how do I know?

Because I am the wife.

And you should always ask the wife.

.

Manifesto:
Here's to the
Presumptuous
Ones

¶∥P

Steve Jobs is often celebrated not just as a technological visionary but as an embodiment of audacity and innovation. His relentless pursuit of excellence and unwavering belief in the power of creativity reshaped industries and changed the world. Jobs didn't just think differently—he lived differently. He saw possibilities where others saw obstacles, and his life's work was a testament to the power of presumptuous thinking and living.

One of my favourite expressions of Jobs' ideology is the "*Here's to the Crazy Ones*" manifesto from Apple's *Think Different* campaign. It wasn't just an advertisement—it was a rallying cry for those who refused to be limited by conventional thinking. It honored the dreamers, the innovators, and the bold thinkers who dared to challenge the status quo and push the boundaries of possibility.

In many ways, the principles in this book mirror those ideals. Living a presumptuous life—one filled with faith, boldness, discipline, and action—is about embracing that same spirit of innovation and fearlessness. It's about daring to believe in the extraordinary and having the courage to pursue it relentlessly.

Inspired by Jobs' manifesto, I felt compelled to create a declaration for this book. Just as *Think Different* inspired a generation of innovators, I hope these words inspire you to live a life of boldness, faith, and purpose.

¶⫿P

Here's to the presumptuous ones. The dreamers. The doers. The overreachers. The ones who don't fit the mold. The ones who see possibilities where others see limits.

They don't play it safe. They have no respect for the status quo. You can admire them or challenge them, celebrate them or question them. But the one thing you can't do is dismiss them.

Because they turn dreams into reality. They push the boundaries of what's possible. And while some may call them presumptuous, we call them audacious.

Because the people who are bold enough to believe they can change their world are the ones who do.

Here's to the ones who take the first step, even when the path isn't clear. The ones who keep their promises, not just to others but to themselves. The ones who turn ideas into action, who rise above fear and doubt, and who embrace the unknown with unwavering faith.

They know that life isn't about waiting for opportunities; it's about creating them. They understand that success is built on a foundation of integrity, faith, and relentless effort. They believe in their God-given potential and pursue their purpose with a tenacity that defies logic.

Here's to the ones who believe in a life of purpose, who trust in the power of their dreams, and who have the courage to live boldly. They don't just survive—they thrive. They inspire. They leave a legacy.

Here's to the presumptuous ones.
The ones who believe in the extraordinary.
The ones who change the world, one presumptuous act at a time.
Here's to You

dlb

Just as Steve Jobs transformed the world with his audacious vision, you can transform your life by embracing the principles in this book.

"The people who are crazy enough to think they can change the world are the ones who do."

This book is a testament to that idea. It's a call to embrace your own crazy, audacious dreams and to pursue them with tenacity and faith.

So here's to you—the presumptuous one.